Ornamental Grasses
for Western Gardens

Ornamental Grasses
for Western Gardens

Marilyn Raff

Johnson Books
Boulder, Colorado

8/2006 GEN FUND $20.00

© 2006 by Marilyn Raff

Published by Johnson Books, a division of Big Earth Publishing,
3005 Center Green Drive, Suite 220, Boulder, Colorado 80301.
E-mail: books@bigearthpublishing.com
www.johnsonbooks.com

Cover and text design by Constance Bollen, cbgraphics

9   8   7   6   5   4   3   2   1

Library of Congress Cataloging-in-Publication Data

Raff, Marilyn.
    Ornamental grasses for western gardens / Marilyn Raff.
        p. cm.
    Includes bibliographical references.
    ISBN 1-55566-369-9
    1. Ornamental grasses—West (U.S.) 2. Arid regions plants—West (U.S.) I.
Title.
    SB431.7.R34 2005
    635.9'3490978—dc22   2005028352

Printed in the United States of America

Dedication

To my father, who loved me,

and to all passionate gardeners around the world

Acknowledgments

Several people assisted me along my garden journey of discovery. Like a bright-eyed child in a candy store, as a learning gardener I was enthusiastic about every new plant or ornamental grass that crossed my path. Kelly Grummons and Panayoti Kelaidis were key players in helping me learn to identify plants and did so willingly, no matter how insignificant my questions appeared.

I have appreciated Leslie Heizer's editing skills in helping me prepare this manuscript, as well as her ongoing interest in ornamental grasses. She taught me the importance of clarity in describing grasses for the novice, as well as for the more advanced gardener.

I am very grateful that, in recent years, I have tapped into a love of the English language. This enthusiasm for words and for reading has empowered me to share with others my enjoyment of flowers. My garden has been my huge research laboratory. Books have given me important information on the growth habits and history of grasses. My own experience of watching so many varieties of ornamental grasses grow and thrive in my garden, and the ways in which I have witnessed them transform from season to season, have helped me bring this book to fruition.

Contents

An Introduction to Ornamental Grasses

Growing up on the East Coast, the only grass I knew was Kentucky bluegrass. I thought of grass only as something to play on. In front of my house we had sloping hills. My friends and I laughed as we rolled down the gentle green mounds, gathering grass clippings on our clothing. In winter, we cared even less about this vegetation, since it was covered over by snow, continually matted down by footprints and the gliding action of the thick metal runners of sleighs.

When I moved to Colorado in later years, I began what would

Korean feather reed grass (Calamagrostis brachytricha) *bonds with black-eyed Susan* (Rudbeckia hirta) *and the fiber-thin stems of tufted hair grass* (Deschampsia cespitosa).

*Blue switch grass (*Panicum virgatum *'Heavy Metal') stands in the forefront
next to the deep, red leaves of nannyberry viburnum (*Viburnum lentago*)
and the wide-open blossoms of Maximilian sunflower.*

evolve into a career in gardening. First, I learned about plantings for rock gardens; next I incorporated perennials and shrub roses. Eventually, I heard positive rumblings from colleagues about ornamental grasses. I looked for them at the garden centers where, stacked off to the side were black pots filled with a few puny stems sticking out. Motivated by curiosity, I began buying some unattractive specimens. However, as these grasses grew and matured, I gradually became hooked. When winds swept through the garden, the attractive seedheads of the grasses quivered. Needless to say, these grasses were entirely different from the manicured green lawn I was accustomed to in my former home in New Jersey. Other than in early spring, when most varieties are cut down and look naked and unappealing, ornamental grasses add a great variety of highlights to the garden. In addition to providing diversity in the garden, many ornamental grasses require little water.

Growing decorative grasses in our gardens—even if only on a small scale—brings back a wild and natural look that for centuries was the predominant feature of the once-vast prairies of the United States. When we use grasses in our gardens we preserve a bit of natural history, uniting ourselves with the great outdoors.

Ornamental grasses can be creatively and easily interwoven with other plants and with many hardscape elements. (Hardscape refers to the nonplant structural elements of the garden, such as flagstone paths, boulders, patios, and fences.) As design elements, the stems, leaves, and clusters of pretty inflorescence on grasses enhance the look of neighboring plants and the overall landscape. The light and airy texture of grasses creates contrast when they are used as a backdrop or alongside a smooth boulder or rock grouping. Grasses are at home near a slow trickle of water, a running stream, or a peaceful pond. Some unique ornamental grasses look best alone, while others can be admired in groupings of two or many.

Most grasses thrive in sunny locations, where the majority of them naturally occur, and they prefer open sites with good air circulation. However, for woody sites there are many ornamental grasses that grow naturally under the canopies of trees. I especially appreciate the many ornamental grasses that have the ability to adapt to arid and semi-arid conditions and thus conserve water for future generations.

I often chuckle that my garden is international, full of roses, grasses, and many perennials that have traveled from far-off lands. Most have been brought to my local garden center, and ultimately my home garden, by explorers and plant collectors who search for awesome, viable new additions for our gardens. This book focuses primarily on the many ornamental grasses I have grown in my home garden over the last fifteen years. My landscape is just over a third of an acre, so I can grow a considerable amount, both large and small. Since installation, care, and maintenance of ornamental grasses are sometimes a mystery to new gardeners, as well as to those who are more experienced, I will help the reader visualize different techniques and approaches to sustaining these valuable plants. In the text and graphs that follow, I share both my enthusiasm for and knowledge of ornamental grasses in the hope that you'll soon discover the wonders of these "plumes with panache."

CHAPTER ONE

Grasses— The Prairie's Hardy Native

O ver the last fifty years, ornamental grasses have come into their own as key plantings in well-designed gardens. Thanks are due a few noteworthy individuals from the past and present who have fostered recognition for these plants, despite the fact that many gardeners once could not envision the beauty and impact ornamental grasses could add to our landscapes.

In Victorian times, grasses were used sparingly in gardens, mostly as individual specimens in a broad swath of turfgrass. In Carol Ottesen's book, *Ornamental Grasses: The Amber*

Two pampas grass (Cortaderia selloana) varieties: 'Andes Silver', the airy, thin one, and 'Patagonia', the fluffy-tipped cultivar.

Giant reed (Arundo donax), *a Mediterranean native,*
may grow more than fourteen feet in a single season in cool temperate regions.

Wave, a black-and-white photo, taken at the Cincinnati Zoo in about 1900, shows a lonely specimen of *Miscanthus* hidden off to the side, tucked in bluegrass, most likely not seen, or ignored by passersby.

Some grasses were sold in garden catalogs in the early 1900s. A 1909 catalog of the Storrs and Harrison Co. of Ohio discusses ornamental grasses in a limited fashion; it focuses on their soft colors, stateliness, and value as an accent to the dominant green of turfgrass. The catalog also mentions the liveliness grasses bring to gardens when winds blow. Selections were limited to *Arundo, Cortaderia, Miscanthus,* and *Pennisetum.* Nowadays, gardeners can choose from a plethora of grasses, as breeders continue to expand the variations in height, texture, color, and style of grasses. As choices increase, more grasses are available for a wide spectrum of climatic conditions and for diverse design schemes.

Karl Foerster (1874–1970) was one of the ornamental grass pioneers. In his gardens in Potsdam-Bornim, Germany, Foerster evaluated plants that he collected from around the world. In the 1940s, he published a catalog that listed 100 types of ornamental grasses. An innovator, he had the brilliant idea to plant grasses among other plants such as aster, helenium, phlox, and salvia. While such integration has become more common-place in recent years, some gardeners still resist this, either opting to be more formal with their designs or not being familiar with how to add ornamental grasses to create a grati-fying visual scene. Occasionally just one or two ornamental grasses can add pizzazz to a

---

A potpourri of plants in late summer divided by a pebbled path. Feather reed grass (Calamagrostis acutiflora 'Karl Foerster') *is dotted throughout. The purple-tipped flower is* Verbena bonariensis; *the sages are 'Silver Frost' and 'Powis Castle'; and other plants include scabiosa, fountain grass, four-wing saltbush, and snapdragons.*

garden scene. But usually, lacking the contrast and partnership of other plants, ornamental grasses, unless planted in profusion, can be a bit dull to look at. When the gardener plants grasses among other plants, an exciting and fruitful union occurs.

Since Karl Foerster first introduced gardeners to grasses and to a more naturalistic planting style, other nurserymen and garden designers have continued to propagate, promote, and sell ornamental grasses. Kurt Bluemel, Inc., located in Baldwin, Maryland, has been in business since 1964, and is one of the premier wholesale nurseries specializing in ornamental grasses, along with other perennials, in our country and around the world. Well-known designers James Van Sweden and Wolfgang Oehme are also famous for popularizing grasses in their installations.

A Brief History of the Bluejoint Turkeyfoot Prairie

The prairie (the term originated in France and referred to grasslands) once comprised vast portions of the midsection of the United States. Originally stretching one thousand miles from east to west and over three thousand miles from north to south, the tallgrass prairie, with its wildflowers and grasses, contained the foundation plantings of the Midwest.

When was this wavy domain discovered? During the American Revolution, the English tried, to no avail, to restrict the colonists from traveling west beyond the Appalachians. The colonies were multiplying fast and began pushing at the boundaries of the forest. What was out there? Many curious and adventuresome folks wanted to see, explore, and perhaps settle in this woodless new territory, whose edges were bordered by immense trees. Geologists, surveyors, and soldiers spread word of the awe-inspiring grasslands, as did the reports from the Lewis and Clark expedition of 1804. In John Madson's excellent book, *Where the Sky Began: Land of the Tallgrass Prairie*, a geologist comments on the beauty of the prairie as it rises along gentle slopes and creates a vista that captures the eye for miles and miles.

For those early intrepid pioneers, the boundaries between the eastern forest and the rising curtain of the Midwest and western plains were blurred as patches of forest and meadow curled in and out of each other. In other places, the tallgrass prairie emerged abruptly from the eastern forests. Coneflower, compass plant, big bluestem, and other prairie plants startled settlers.

Once a dominant plant of the tallgrass prairie, *Andropogon gerardii* (big bluestem) reached heights of five to eight feet. Also called "bluejoint turkeyfoot" because of its distinctive tri-branched seedheads, this grass looked like a frail but upside-down turkey

*Blue grama (*Bouteloua gracilis*), little bluestem (*Schizachyrium scoparium*), along with other native grasses and beard tongue (*Penstemon grandiflorus*), in summer.*

foot. Since portions of the Midwest had adequate moisture, *Spartina pectinata* (prairie cord grass) also thrived (this grass is native to bogs and wet soils).

Today, 99 percent of the original tallgrass prairie has been cultivated as farmland. The prairie, with its well-drained, fertile soil and exposure to full sun, provided ideal conditions for growing corn and other edibles such as wheat, barley, and oats. It took years for these agricultural plants to become established. Initially settlers painstakingly

ABOVE: *As autumn shuffles in, little bluestem (Schizachyrium scoparium) seems to stand guard alongside a weeping spruce.*

BELOW: *The russet color of little bluestem (Schizachyrium scoparium) and the soft, unbleached seedheads of blue grama (Bouteloua gracilis) are a distinctive combination.*

plowed the sod, broke it, and weakened it so that it would gradually decompose and, once tilled a few times, be ready to receive fresh seed.

Where conditions were drier, throughout the windswept Great Plains and abutting the Rocky Mountains, miles and miles of short-grass prairie thrived. This prairie extended roughly from Canada to Texas, into regions of Nebraska, Kansas, and eastern Colorado. Here hail, snow, sun, and rain might all pass through in a matter of days or even hours! Howling winds were a strong factor in drying plants out quickly and severely restricting their height. To survive, plants had to adapt by hanging low, and many did. Instead of the tall billowing grasses and wildflowers of the tallgrass prairie, plants low in stature, such as *Bouteloua gracilis* (blue grama) and *Schizachyrium scoparium* (little bluestem) adapted to the harsh conditions of the Great Plains. Other plants that adapted well to the short-grass prairie were sedums with their succulent stems, sages known for their silvery filigree foliage, and various plants whose long taproots helped them conserve water, such as *Callirhoe involucrata* (poppy mallow or wine cups). I grow many of these native species in my Littleton, Colorado, garden, which, I am fond of thinking, connects me to the brave pioneers and explorers of earlier times.

Grasses in the Midwest and on the rugged landscape of the Great Plains acclimated, in part, because of their deep, fibrous root system. While floods, rain, and hail ravaged the prairie, wreaking havoc with top growth, the underground root network, like a heavy anchor, stabilized the soil. This characteristic enabled plants to survive harsh climatic conditions. According to extensive research done by Neil Diboll, owner of Prairie Nursery in Westfield, Wisconsin, approximately 70 percent of the average prairie plant is roots, while the leaves and other foliage amount to only about one-third of the total plant material. Some prairie plants, such as prairie cord grass, have roots that travel to a depth of twenty feet, which enables them to easily survive adverse conditions above ground. In addition, as roots decay, they become compost or organic matter that naturally enriches the soil.

In nature, grasses rarely grow alone. On the open prairie, meadow, or mountain terrain, grasses are a substantial part of a unique and complex ecosystem, made up of wildflowers, alpine plants, organic matter (detritus, leaves, fungus, plant parts, and soil), and inorganic elements (stones and minerals), as well as various large and small animals. When grasslands disappear, plants that coexist with the grasses are also eliminated. For example, *Hypoxis hirsuta* (yellow stargrass) is a rare grass that once grew amply in moist portions of the short-grass prairie. This two-foot-tall grass is still seen

*Little bluestem (*Schizachyrium scoparium*) near fernbush (*Chamaebatiaria millefolium*) in fall.*

frequently in the Midwest, East, and South, but has only been reported five times in the past one hundred years in Colorado. In California as well as other states, when native grasses are erased, so are choice bulbs and wildflowers, which need each other to thrive. In earlier centuries, when California wildflowers such as California poppies and lupines bloomed exuberantly, ships heading home from their long travels away would be guided by the bright colors of these flowers, as if by a lighthouse, to their destinations.

Grasses, as well as other flowers, provide food for wildlife, such as for insects, butterflies, and birds. In addition, these natural wild sites are home to larger mammals such as squirrels, deer, or prairie dogs, the latter of which like to wiggle through short grasses. (Prairie dogs are regarded by some as a pest. I think they are up to a point. However, they were initially an intrinsic part of the ecosystem of drier grasslands. Because of their burrowing activities, prairie dogs reduce soil compaction, increase the soil's ability to absorb water, and serve as a major food source for small animals like eagles, foxes, and owls.) Beyond the habitat grasses offer for wildlife, they add bulk and form to any landscape. After the coming chill of winter zaps wildflowers late in the fall, many grasses continue upright, extending the seasonal beauty of the prairie with splashes of color, texture, and form.

The J. C. Raulston Arboretum at North Carolina State University is a famous garden, and offers a breathtaking scene using ornamental grasses. I remember years ago seeing how the arboretum made excellent use of this up-and-coming plant material. Planted along one deep border, among the many hundreds of perennials, were dozens of decorative grasses. Late in fall, the wind blasted through the border, rustling the grasses and invigorating the flowers. The movement reminded me of a herd of galloping horses whose pounding, heavy feet stir up dust and plants along their path. When I first saw this border, one of the arboretum's gardeners had upped the ante by spraypainting, in a horizontal manner, the tawny stems and plumes of the grasses in shades of orange, blue, and red. I'm sure this creative act tempted garden visitors to take note and purchase grasses upon their return home.

On my home turf, in the Denver Botanic Gardens, ornamental grasses are used in various creative ways; some are mixed in with perennials. In several places, other more drought-tolerant species, such as *Bouteloua gracilis* (blue grama) and *Bouteloua curtipendula* (side-oats grama), are massed together to punctuate the presence of stout evergreens. The panorama is especially picturesque on sunny, cold winter days when gardeners seek out any glowing plant arrangement to lift their spirits while waiting impatiently for spring.

The Truth About Grass Growth Habits

A few ornamental grasses spread quickly via underground runners, causing mischief as their roots creep into areas where they are not welcome. These running grasses can quickly take over in a flower bed, spoiling the reputation of the better-behaved grasses—of which there are many. Homeowners may have tried a particularly rambunctious grass, which spread like a tidal wave, choking out desirable plants and ruining the intended look of the garden. Having experienced the damage of one invasive grass, some people have banned grasses permanently from their plots of land.

There is no need for such a ban! Clump-forming grasses stay more compact and are easier to control. Both running and clump-forming grasses are appropriate for a garden setting *if the right plant is used in the right place*. A grass that will become invasive in a particular spot can be ideal in another. For example, with firm barriers—perhaps a cement or stone sidewalk—*Phalaris arundinacea picta* (ribbon grass) stays where it is planted. Where there is a slope or other difficult-to-design area, ribbon grass may provide a solution. I have also seen it spruce up a patio when used as an annual in a barrel encircled by trailing vines and colorful annuals. But ribbon grass in a perennial border creates big trouble. New gardeners often purchase this grass for its lovely green and white foliage. "How darling," one thinks, "I'll put it in front of such and such a plant." Soon the ribbon grass invades a few choice flower beds and needs to be removed entirely.

When I teach classes on grasses, I hear horror stories about ribbon grass and its roving habit. Environment, too, plays a significant role with fast-spreading grasses. Inventive gardeners limit their watering of grasses and/or plant them in heavier clay soils to curtail the weedy temperament of grasses that tend to spread vigorously. The best solution to potential grass problems is to be informed about the grass you purchase and to choose the right place to plant it. Check with knowledgeable nursery staff or read about ornamental grasses before buying, and your grass experience will be more positive.

Most of the grasses I describe in this book are clump forming. These grasses form dense mounds and are easily managed when it is necessary to weed around them or move them (although some muscle may be required to lift and divide mature grasses). While clump-forming grasses generally stay put, the wind and birds do disperse seeds. After approximately six to ten years, some clump-forming grasses may pop up in other spots in your garden. Is this a problem, or is it a gift to the gardener? In most cases I call it a gift. Perhaps you like where the grass has settled. If a few extra plants have moved in, you can easily dig them up and move them to another spot. In addition you can give them away, something I have done repeatedly for fellow gardeners who have admired the grass in my garden.

Grasslike Plants

Botanically speaking, grasses belong to the Gramineae (also known as Poaceae) family. In addition to true grasses, there are plants that do not belong to either one of these families but look very much like grasses because of their repetitive linear form. Among these, I adore *Ophiopogon planiscapus* 'Nigrescens' (black mondo grass) for its graceful growth habit and foliage color. This plant belongs to the lily family (Lilium), but is a close look-alike for a dark-colored grass. Some *Yucca* varieties have a bulkier form than grasses, but they are eye-catching with their daggerlike appearance and linear shapes,

*Sprays of ribbon grass (*Phalaris arundinacea picta*)
combine with 'Six Hills Giant' catmint (*Nepeta × faassenii *'Six Hills Giant'*).*

---

and so in a broad sense, this puts them in the same neighborhood as grasses. *Yucca glauca* (soapweed), a native plant of the Rocky Mountain region, is quite dramatic when viewed against clouds that float in an ocean-blue sky. Another grass-like plant is *Luzula sylvatica* (greater woodrush). I obtained the plant because my garden guru, the late Graham Stuart Thomas, one of the most esteemed horticulturists of the twentieth

The arrowlike flowers and pointy green leaves of soapweed
(Yucca glauca) make a striking picture against an ocean-blue sky.

century, was a fan of this particular woodland plant. These plants are rushes, which belong to the Juncaceae family. Finally, varieties of *Carex* (sedges), from the family Cyperaceae, provide a grasslike appearance in an enchanting range of colors, from coppery shades to jade green to variegated hues.

I include many of these grasslike plants in this book. I also devote space to a smattering of annual grasses because a few fetching ones have caught my attention. However, I mostly favor the ease of perennial grasses, which require simple once-a-year cutting and occasional division, providing marvelous features with minimal care.

Ornamental Grasses—Drought-Tolerant Plants

In the world of horticulture, the word "drought" can be a bombshell. It can shock people into realizing that puffy but often dry white clouds lead to shrinking reservoirs that can't keep up with the never-ending call for water. In many regions of our country, limited water supply is met with increased demand, particularly as more people move

Black mondo grass (Ophiopogon planiscapus 'Nigrescens').

into areas once less populous. In my state of Colorado in the year 2002, 20,000 people moved in, with another 20,000 arriving in 2003. As municipalities brainstorm the problem of water scarcity, trying to find solutions that are equitable for everyone in terms of water restrictions and usage guidelines, gardeners find themselves experiencing everything from concern to panic.

A blessing for gardeners during dry times comes in the form of drought-tolerant plants. A range of spectacular plants adapt well to dry and challenging conditions. In 2002 the Rocky Mountain region suffered the worst drought in hundreds of years. During that sizzling summer, sales were sluggish. In the fall, however, certain plants, mostly xeric, sold out.

The following year, on March 18 and 19, 2003, the largest blizzard since December 1913 smacked into the area, dumping three to seven feet (the variation in depth of the snow depended on which section of the region you lived in) of heavy wet snow on large portions of Colorado and Wyoming, from the foothills to the plains! Gardeners were extremely grateful and hoped water limitations would be modified. Although the spring of 2003 continued to bring more moisture to the region, water restrictions were altered only slightly. Summer watering was restricted to twice a week, with absolutely no watering between 10 A.M. and 6 P.M. Steep surcharges were tacked onto water bills for single-family households using more than 18,000 gallons in a two-month period, regardless of the number of people in the household or size of the landscape. The promotion and sales of xeric plants were on the rise and by the summer of 2003, management at Denver Water (the region's water management agency) gave people discounts for installing xeric plants. Since that time, despite improvements in the region's water supply, the lasting lesson for consumers is that water must be conserved—and water-wise or xeriscape plantings are a key element in doing so.

Grasses, along with certain perennials and low-growing rock garden plants, are the heroes of the ongoing, often challenging battle with Mother Nature that gardeners in the West face. (Recently, even gardeners in the East have faced droughts!) Gardeners who live in western states need to be obstinate folks, ready to persevere when environmental disasters strike our cherished gardens.

Because ornamental grasses have extremely solid root systems, it takes a lot to expunge them. They have fiercely held their ground for centuries, which is probably why I have rarely, if ever, lost an ornamental grass! While trees and shrubs bring structure, flowers, and leaves to the garden, grasses offer both their beauty and a bit of insurance in the face of unpredictable weather.

Our most common turf, Kentucky bluegrass, is a water hog. While the emerald-green lawn it creates is viable back east or in sections of the country where water is more abundant, in drier regions such grass needs to be replaced, or at least given less water—which it can survive. For greatest success, gardeners should work in harmony with the land. Where moisture is low, install appropriate plants. Where moisture is more plentiful, install plants that thrive under those conditions. For people living on the Great Plains, where dry conditions are the norm, it is most prudent to install plants that can prosper with minimal additions of moisture. Be water thrifty. I feel fortunate that my small plot of land is situated at the bottom of a steep slope. From several different angles I get water runoff, which is helpful during hot summers and when drought conditions predominate.

Thomas Christopher, author of *Water-Wise Gardening: America's Backyard Revolution*, writes about various ground covers for low-water situations. While researching his book, he toured thirty gardens throughout the country, talking with gardeners in various states. He was shocked as he saw gardeners in Phoenix, Arizona, literally flooding their landscapes during hot spells (which in Phoenix is practically all the time) to keep their grass green in the midst of a desert. Christopher also describes feeling uplifted when he came upon gardens in Santa Barbara, California, and Denver, Colorado, where innovative gardeners lavished their gardens with color, texture, and form, while carefully controlling the amount of water they poured on their gardens.

During times of water shortages, gardeners and the landscaping industry receive lowest priority for water use. In the February/March 2003 issue of the *Colorado Gardener*, local garden writer and nursery owner Mikl Brawner stated: "According to many water utilities, water use is prioritized like this: 1) indoor water use is defined as essential (*regardless of inefficiency and waste*); 2) business water use is defined as essential (*includes car washes, bottling companies and golf courses*); 3) landscaping is defined as nonessential (*regardless of the impact on related businesses and homeowner's investments in landscape*)." The italicized comments are Mr. Brawner's. It is interesting to note that the water needs of golf courses, car washes, and bottling companies are considered more essential than those for people who work in horticulture or who garden.

As a matter of perception, it doesn't help the cause of the horticulture industry and committed gardeners when passersby see sprinkler water streaming down curbs, sidewalks, and streets—all in the cause of keeping a bluegrass lawn eternally green in an arid environment. Surprisingly, during recent drought conditions, newspapers were

Little bluestem (Schizachyrium scoparium) in late summer.

flooded with articles about appropriate plants for dry regions and how to handle a parched landscape, but grasses were scarcely mentioned. Is it because the plumes of these grasses are not as bountiful and richly endowed as the flowers of other plants? Or are most people unfamiliar with this refreshing plant material? I think it is a combination of both.

People who have lived in a region for an extended length of time are familiar with the natural look of the land. Some readily adapt to it, while others fight it. For decades, it has been fashionable to take pride in weedless, bouncy green lawns, a look for which many yet strive. Now we must change!

Ornamental grasses and water-wise plants are major ingredients of a change in this perception. Whether conditions are moist or dry, soils are sandy or clayey, grasses adjust to a wide spectrum of conditions with minimal care required. Well-known garden writer Allen Lacy quips, "The main thing to do with ornamental grasses is to watch them grow and change through the season."

The average gardener may still feel mystified by ornamental grasses. Why grow them? What can they offer to the landscape? Breeders, plant explorers, nursery owners, and other horticulture professionals are doing their part by spreading the word about alternatives to bluegrass and creating new, enticing varieties for our gardens. Gardeners are finding ever more grasses at garden centers—both varieties brought from abroad and native varieties being rediscovered. As gardeners discover the delights of these grasses and request them, breeders take note and, over time, introduce even more grasses into the market.

The following chapter deals with the all-important matter of how grasses look. Beyond their water-wise qualities and easy care, grasses can provide powerful visual impact in a garden. Their appealing continuous, repetitive lines and fluid movement are often the things that ignite a passion for ornamental grasses.

CHAPTER TWO

The Beauty of Ornamental Grasses

When ornamental grasses are planted in private gardens or massed in a public arena, their powerful shapes catch the eye of gardeners and garden visitors alike. Their appearance differs considerably from the look of most other plants. Distinct, ongoing lines are a potent feature of all grasses and many grasslike plants, no matter their color, size, or shape. Whether you simply putter in the garden on weekends or passionately attend to your flowers with no regard to time spent, grasses are plants that resonate. Imagine this scenario: It's late fall and you and a friend are

---

*Toward summer's end, goldenrod (*Solidago altissima*) accents the fluffy plumes of fountain grass (*Pennisetum alopecuroides*).*

driving along a city street. Suddenly, you're magnetized by the stately bearing and parchment color of an ornamental grass. You're not too familiar with this plant, but admire the look, and say to your friend, "I like that rocketlike appearance!" Suddenly, you slow down to give the plant a more meaningful once-over. Next you're wondering out loud, "How can I fit this exquisite specimen into my garden next spring?"

One aesthetic bonus of ornamental grasses is the way they change appearance throughout the year. Often they start out green. Then their plumes in shades of beige or maroon gradually reach upward, some wide, some narrow, and others adorned with extremely fine-textured inflorescences, such as in the case of *Deschampsia cespitosa* (tufted hair grass). In fall and winter, grasses take center stage, like a dramatic star. This may at first seem peculiar to the new gardener or to those who have been drawn to gardening for the spring to late-summer extravaganza of color. I heartily concur with Rick Darke, editor of *The New Royal Horticultural Society Dictionary Manual of Grasses* when he declares, "The rigors of winter fail to diminish the beauty of ornamental grasses: in the opinion of most gardeners, this is their peak season."

Ornamental grasses have different cycles; those in winter and fall last the longest. Growth stops in late fall, but grasses maintain their shape and continue to evolve in terms of flower and leaf color. Each of these cycles, no matter how brief, either boldly or subtly contributes to the way grasses punctuate the garden with their distinctive personalities. Just as people change from day to day, month to month, and year to year—but simultaneously stay the same at core—grasses behave in a similar vein.

From spring to late fall, grasses offer fresh delights. In late April, weeks after I've cut down all my grasses, I sigh with delight as pointy green shoots ever so gently emerge from the hollow cylindrical stalks and old leaves left from the previous season. Change can also be seen in the panicles (flower clusters) of a particular *Miscanthus*. One year they are off-white and fluffy; the next, because of a chilly fall or other variables such as sun, water, and shade, their coloring might be taupe. A few individual plumes of an unnamed *Miscanthus* may be twisty like a corkscrew one year, and the next year stretched out lax and thin.

If moisture is not sufficient in a given year, *Panicum* (switch grass) and *Pennisetum* (fountain grass) may not produce pleasing plumage. Even without its plumage, the half-inch-wide steel-blue leaves of some *Panicum*, when gathered in clumps, move in the breeze with the pulsating rhythm of a heartbeat. In my garden, the plant's droopy leaves rest on the scattered red and gray stones beneath it. This creates a carefree scene, enhanced further when the faded ivory balls of the two-foot-tall *Allium caeruleum* bend onto the blue foliage. If fountain grass does not bloom, its fan-shaped form and light

Hardy pampas grass (Saccharum ravennae) *dominates the landscape
when surrounded by muted tones of fall, such as the reddish bunches of joe-pye weed*
(Eupatorium purpureum maculatum *'Gateway') and the light-colored foliage
of variegated Japanese silver grass* (Miscanthus sinensis *'Variegatus').*

green color are sufficient to enthrall the gardener. Luckily, however, through occasional autumns in my garden, the foliage of fountain grass has shimmered burnt orange.

Certain grasses may be visually dominating. The flower clusters of *Panicum virgatum* 'Dallas Blues' (switch grass) are large and robust. In contrast, the light-as-a-feather plumes of *Deschampsia cespitosa* (tufted hair grass) are quietly spectacular. *Bouteloua curtipendula* (side-oats grama) is adorned with threadlike spears that gather only along one side of the stem, creating an unusual, asymmetrical beauty. The intriguing floral display of *Bouteloua gracilis* (blue grama), also known as eyelash grass, does indeed look like eyelashes.

In addition to the diverse flowers that grow from the upper portion of most grasses, the foliage or leaves below often have an impact on our senses. Structurally, the foliage, along with the roots, helps to secure the plant; visually, it adds mounds of various textures and colors.

Feather reed grass (Calamagrostis acutiflora *'Karl Foerster'*)
produces a willowy head of plumes and is framed by fourwing saltbush (Atriplex canescens)
and the blue-green leaves of blue allium (Allium caeruleum*)*.

Grass leaves may be very finely textured, as in the case of certain *Muhlenbergia*, which is an excellent grass choice for semiarid and arid regions. Some grasses are adorned with three-inch-wide thick leaves, as is *Arundo donax* (giant reed). This grass, originating in southern Europe, was brought to the New World by Spanish colonizers and was instrumental in home construction for the early settlers. Once the stalks were dried, the canes were used for roofs and animal corrals, thus protecting settlers from the elements and wild animals.

The foliage of some grasses is extremely vertical, as in the ever-popular *Calamagrostis acutiflora* 'Karl Foerster' (feather reed grass), or it may angle outward as do varieties of *Miscanthus*. Other grasses, including blue fescues, are low-growing bunch types, which dot the landscape in much-loved shades of blue and buff. The combination of grasses' vertical lines and striking plumage makes for endless glory in the garden.

Whether in a perennial border, xeric garden, or shrub planting, ornamental grasses exhilarate a garden as they reach skyward, quivering at the slightest breath of air. When winds blow briskly, my garden becomes uproarious with swells of movement and sound. Grasses are the only plant material to offer this uncommon drama. Other plants may move in the wind, but they do not feature the consistent repeating lines of grasses, which augment the visual glamour.

This glamour is magnified when the grasses' fall shades of beige—which often include muted orange, tan, and off-white—plus its airy plumes contrast with neighboring plants. In particular the straight lines of the four- to five-foot-tall feather reed grass add vibrancy to a scene when they glide through the curved stems of 'Applejack' roses or other plants. Mixing the stems of any variety of shrub rose with the plumes of grass and the opposite textures of both, thorny against soft, creates an attractive scenario.

Harmony and Contrast

Harmony and contrast are the name of the game with grasses. Mix and mingle grasses with other plants or hardscape elements and their magnificent display is upgraded many notches. Decorating the garden is akin to interior design, only with living

In the summer, feather reed grass (Calamagrostis acutiflora 'Karl Foerster')
helps accentuate 'Nymphenburg' rose, while Persian yellow rose covers a fence.

The tan plumage of feather reed grass (Calamagrostis acutiflora *'Karl Foerster'*)
takes center stage near the yellow blossoms of false sunflower (Heliopsis helianthoides)
and the blossoms of a mini-rose.

specimens. Interior decorators are concerned with color matching, coordinating, and contrast with regard to furniture, artifacts, colors, and textures. Some people spend days, weeks, or months researching paint. Do I want glossy or flat, sky-blue, red, or eggshell on the walls? And what of the texture for the sofa—will it be velvet, leather, or corduroy—smooth or ribbed?

When choosing grasses for the garden, similar choices of color and texture must be made. I rub the stalks or plumes between my fingers to gauge how the grass feels—smooth or rough? I choose grasses for many reasons and from many sources: I may find a certain grass in a book or catalog, or the foliage color may strike my fancy when I shop at the nursery. With any grass, I imagine how it might look throughout the year, envisioning all the seasonal changes. As my grasses thrive and expand and I need to move and/or divide them, I look for gaps in my borders where a tall, cushiony, or springy-looking grass might create a charming new scene.

Designing outside has the added factor of weather—snow, rain, sun, shade, wind, and more. Some winter mornings, frost will trace the outline of grasses. I like the effect of gleaming white snow against shades of tan and green. After a mild snowstorm, I look out my office window and watch the snow disappear from the sheaths of grasses and slowly, as the sun beats down on the grasses, they rise up again. Grasses in shade create a cooling, restful spot.

Most flowers, when knitted among grasses or planted near them, create pleasant scenes that show off all the plants. Here is one example of a beautiful flower combination. It's early summer. As I walk along my flagstone path, my eyes gravitate toward a trio of plants: the imposing pastel flowers of *Eremurus* × *isabellinus* (desert candle or foxtail lily); tall, ribbon-pink snapdragons; and *Helictotrichon sempervirens* (blue oat grass), with its thin, powdery blue lines. The colors, textures, and variations in height of these plants create a fine composition. Some of my planting schemes are done purposefully. But most, like the one described above, are planted together on a whim. I've spent

---

*Desert candle (*Eremurus *sp.) adds sparkle in front of the opening leaves of blue oat grass (*Helictotrichon sempervirens*).*

many years learning the forms and blooming patterns of plants and now feel free to take chances with design. If I'm not pleased with the composition I've dreamed up, most plants can be moved easily.

In one spot I have two feather reed grasses planted a few yards away from a pea-gravel path, which is lined in curved red bricks. These grasses look like wheat-colored steeples against the blue and white skyline. Closer to the path is *Bromus benekenii* (brome grass). This three-foot-high grass, planted along a curve, very close to the bricks and in front of the feather reed grass, has green stems in summer, with attractive wispy tan tips that gently weep down. The entire picture invites tranquillity into the garden. In addition, *Bromus benekenii*, whose color matches the feather reed grass, turns strong tones of orange in fall. Its drooping habit is an ideal mate for the soldierlike architectural structure of the feather reed grass. The brome grass spreads moderately underground by creeping rhizomes, but since I'm immensely fond of its fluid nature, I'm willing to deal with this flaw, attending to the extra weeding. In fall and winter, *Picea*

Clumps of brome grass (Bromus benekenii) *engulf the purple stalks of* Phlomis alpina *and the candy-pink blossoms of 'Nymphenburg' rose.*

The fine-spun fall stems of brome grass (Bromus benekenii)
sway in front of 'Professor Kippenburg' aster.

———————

pungens 'Globosa' (dwarf Colorado blue spruce), vibrant with sharp blue needles, accentuates the view from my back door. It's a pleasant sight as small gray flickers play aerial tag around the spruce.

Even though I tolerate the extra weeding I must do to grow *Bromus benekenii*, it is the only brome I willingly grow in my garden. My garden backs up to a greenbelt where *Bromus inermis* (smooth broom) is the dominant common weed, which is prevalent across much of the United States. This unwelcome guest creeps into my flower beds, and I often need to pull a foot or two of root to completely remove it! The struggle is especially irksome when smooth brome wiggles its way into the middle of a mature clump of blue avena grass. It interferes with the stunning all-embracing blue cast of the avena. These two bromes keep me so busy that, when I see *Bromus inermis* 'Skinner's Gold'— known for its lovely yellow variegated summer coloring—for sale at a local garden center, I avoid it, thinking that in a few short years it would require even more weeding

ABOVE: *The pale yellow flowers of 'Golden Wings' rose peek through the beige tassels and variegated leaves of feather reed grass 'Overdam'* (Calamagrostis acutiflora 'Overdam').
BELOW LEFT: *In summer, the crisp white flowers of an unknown dianthus complement the lax green leaves of Korean feather reed grass* (Calamagrostis brachytricha).
BELOW RIGHT: *In fall, 'Autumn Joy' sedum emerges through the puffy, pink-tinged leaves of Korean feather reed grass* (Calamagrostis brachytricha).

work. Of course weeding goes along with gardening, but in my garden I can set my limits—and no more brome!

If I want yellow coloration in the garden, I'm happy to purchase *Calamagrostis acutiflora* 'Overdam' (feather reed grass 'Overdam'), whose vertical leaves are striped cream-white and green. This grass has plumage similar to the common feather reed grass, although overall it is slightly shorter. 'Overdam' sits at the bottom of a small hill in front of the shrub rose 'Golden Wings'. As the years have passed, the canes of the rose have gotten thick, like bamboo, with many thorns. The single yellow flowers of the rose, together with the delicate nature of the thin grass, soften the look of the rose's menacing canes.

When winds kick up in my garden, I like the swaying motion of the four-foot-tall *Calamagrostis brachytricha* (Korean feather reed grass). Its soft, flame-shaped inflorescences, which feel like a cat's tail, ignite the flower border with their faint purple plumes. The flowers appear in September and slowly fade to an alluring, almost ghostly white; they remain standing through most winters. For an effective scene, plant *C. brachytricha* in small or large groupings. Mine are situated near the silvery-white mounds of *Artemisia* 'Powis Castle' (wormwood) and the crinkly mid-green leaves of *Sidalcea* 'Party Girl' (prairie mallow), whose long-lasting summer flowers, on three- to four-foot stems, are a colorful candy pink.

As its common name states, Korean feather reed grass grows wild in a moist woodland setting on the Korean peninsula. But it also succeeds in somewhat dry conditions. This grass thrives in partial shade beneath deciduous trees. Try Korean feather reed grass in this situation, or partner it up with shrub roses in full sun. The pale autumn coloring of this grass would look stylish next to the shiny and plump apple-red hips of any white rose. A real bonus for me is the way shaggy but attractive Korean feather reed grass looks in June, before its puffy plumes appear. At this stage, when the plant is a foot high, its shimmering sea-green leaves create a vignette near the porcelain-white dianthus.

Color in My Garden, published in 1918 by Louise Beebe Wilder, discusses the effusive elegance that comes about when roses are incorporated among grasses. I make repeated use of this technique. When the rose 'Morden Ruby' is planted close to *Deschampsia cespitosa* (tufted hair grass), for instance, its deep burgundy canes are highlighted beautifully. The grass's green foliage and refined pale, wheat-colored silky plumes seem to flutter through the dark-colored rough canes of the rose, blending opposite textures and colors into a pleasing montage.

As cool fall weather approaches, the yielding crest of Korean feather reed grass (Calamagrostis brachytricha) *contrasts with the prickly florets of false sea holly* (Eryngium planum).

Tufted hair grass forms sturdy clumps and grows well in full sun or lightly shaded areas. In too much shade, its flowers are less profuse. Plant one as a specimen or plant a half dozen or so in sweeps to create a meadowy effect or add bulk to the setting. Although tufted hair grass is found naturally in meadows or moist areas throughout the Northern Hemisphere, some forms are drought-tolerant. I have found that to be the case with this grass. Plant tufted hair grass among bold granite rocks. Enjoy the contrast between the dense and colorful stone and the ethereal plumes of the grass. Although it is helpful with grasses, as well as with other plants, to know their natural growing conditions, you can experiment and adapt the grass to growing conditions in your own garden. Since tufted hair grass is an early bloomer, it is a great mate for the bountiful blooms of roses. Plant this grass next to hardy roses that bloom once in June or repeat bloom in summer and fall. In addition to admiring the texture of the grass against the rose stems in fall and winter, you will be charmed by the unique arrangement when the golden plumes bond with the round and colorful form of any rose.

I relish the chance to approach grasses, to see, touch, and listen to them as they wind through masses of various perennials such as the popular *Knautia macedonica*, with its small, button-sized dark red flowers, or the daisy blooms of *Rudbeckia hirta* (black-eyed Susan).

Hemerocallis (daylily) is an easy-to-grow perennial that I have used as a companion plant with ornamental grasses. Near a dense mound of hair grass called *Deschampsia flexuosa* (crinkled hair grass)—which is not terribly crinkled, rather its plumes are slightly wavy—an unknown daylily sparkles with bright gold-orange flowers and dense foliage. This daylily acts as an attractive backdrop for the billowy, whitish panicles of the crinkled hair grass. The grass's wire-thin foliage is shiny green like a scallion and symmetrical in form. When in flower, crinkled hair grass is almost two feet high and wide. It is comfortable growing in dry shade as well as full sun. I have admired its elegance in a dry cobblestone streambed. In this setting, in fall, its light coffee-colored seedheads are surrounded by the greenery of other plants, creating pleasant contrast. When I clip this

Tufted hair grass (Deschampsia cespitosa) *and 'Morden Ruby' rose envelop the wide-open flowers of black-eyed Susan* (Rudbeckia hirta).

LEFT: *Puffy foliage of tufted hair grass (*Deschampsia cespitosa*) mixes with the frothy leafage of 'Powis Castle' artemisia.*

RIGHT: *A picturesque woodland view captures the round formation of tufted hair grass (*Deschampsia cespitosa*) as it contrasts with the vertical lines and pockmarks of aging aspen trees.*

---

grass down in late winter, I enjoy shaping it like a half-moon, then running my hands across the dome, feeling the sharp strawlike texture of the remaining stalks.

Planted behind the hair grass and daylily is a plant I truly cherish for average or moist spots—the imposing *Eupatorium purpureum maculatum* 'Gateway' (joe-pye weed). At five or six feet tall, it makes an excellent frame for the daylily and the crinkled hair grass in late summer, when its cauliflower-sized maroon flowers attractively tower above the grass and the daylily.

Deschampsia cespitosa 'Fairy's Joke' (tufted hair grass 'Fairy's Joke'), sometimes known as *Deschampsia cespitosa* var. *vivipara*, grows under practically any conditions. Although this lax-looking grass spreads quickly in loose soils, I keep it because I like the unusual tiny plantlets on the flower spikes. These tangled masses of weeping green tentacles, more than a foot long, touch and drag on the ground, often weighing down the entire plant. Sometimes forming tiers, the plantlets bond with the soil and often start new plants. I originally planted this grass in a section of my garden where the soil was heavily amended, so I moved it to a spot with less amendment where it will not travel so quickly.

A tufted hair grass that has grown reliably for me for a number of years is *Deschampsia cespitosa* 'Bronzeschleier' ('Bronze Veil' tufted hair grass). This dense two-foot-wide clump reaches two and a half feet high when its feathery bronze-green flowers appear. It divides easily and recovers quickly when replanted, thus producing more 'Bronze Veil' to decorate my garden. Blooms begin in June. It's an excellent mate to many shrub roses. Soaring behind my 'Bronze Veil' is the onetime-blooming rose 'Hebe's Lip', which grows to five feet and has intense prickly thorns. I don't get too close to this rose; I just stand back and take satisfaction in its creamy-white fragrant flowers, which are scarlet at the tip. When gusts of wind pass through, the plumes of the grass get snarled like flies in a spider's web among the rose canes.

As much as I feel drawn toward shrub roses and grasses, I also like my garden to display diverse plant choices. When I saw *Physocarpus opulifolius* 'Diabolo' ('Diabolo' ninebark), a new shrub on the market a while back, I knew I could find a place for it. It appealed to me because of its three-lobed, reddish plum leaves, whose shape was akin to a maple leaf. Six years later, the shrub is close to maturity at four feet high and wide. It makes an elegant companion in back of the 'Bronze Veil' grass. The older stems of the

The herb borage, the red-buttoned flowers of Knautia macedonica, *and 'Morden Ruby' rose keep company with the faint, yellow-tipped leaves of tufted hair grass (*Deschampsia cespitosa*).*

Crinkled hair grass (Deschampsia flexuosa) *sparkles near assorted perennials such as daylilies and the burgundy crownlike flowers of joe-pye weed* (Eupatorium purpureum maculatum *'Gateway').*

ninebark are coarse and corky tan, and new growth is muted red. The strong features of this shrub make it a "just right" choice to partner near any grass whose leaves are a relaxed green.

Deschampsia cespitosa 'Northern Lights' (tufted hair grass 'Northern Lights') has variegated green and white leaves, sometimes with tints of pink. My specimen had those colors the first few years, but then the variegation disappeared, which I learned sometimes happens. This diminutive species, one foot tall and two feet wide, has straight, fan-shaped leaves that appear like a dense crown. My plants were slow to produce flowers—it took them about four years. These thread-thin ivory and golden plumes, which have a faint twist to them when examined closely, come on the scene in early summer and grow in height an additional eight inches or so. At the base of the grass, I've planted clumps of spicy fragrant deep rouge dianthus. When I pass this spot, I stoop down, rub the plumes of the grass between my fingers, and smile as I inhale the strong scent of the dianthus.

In the vicinity of the dianthus, try the popular grass *Pennisetum alopecuroides* (fountain grass). The plant's common name speaks to its arching habit. I'm fond of its wide-open posture, reaching four feet high and wide. Foliage color begins as gentle green and as fall emerges transforms into a brocade of burnt orange, steely blue, and green. The plant produces a floral display in late summer, which lasts well into fall. Its spongy-looking flowers, sometimes creamy white or pale pink, are dramatic because there are so many of them on a single plant. The three- to four-inch-long blooms are springy. In late fall, if you grasp the plant just beneath its blooms and pull upward, the child within you will take pleasure in scattering the flower parts far and wide!

Fountain grass prefers full sun, but will flourish in partial shade too. I have various perennial forms scattered throughout my garden. When fountain grass is planted in quantity, such as at Longwood Gardens in Kennett Square, Pennsylvania, it creates a grand focus. One fall I saw many along a path with a long red brick and lattice fence in the background. The repetitions of the green grasses with their long narrow leaves loosened the look of the solid stone.

<hr />

Among the stones and greenery of the Denver Botanic Gardens' Rock Alpine Garden, crinkled hair grass (Deschampsia flexuosa) *is luminous.*

*In fall, the tips of fountain grass (*Pennisetum alopecuroides)*
fade to a wheat color as the red foliage of a currant shrub stands out in the background.*

On a smaller scale, I have one fountain grass that seems to erupt like a mini-volcano, then appears to float over a low, rugged-looking rock wall. Around the grass and stuck in the jagged crevices of the wall, I impulsively planted silver thyme and a few unnamed *Sempervivum* (hen and chicks). The intricate texture and plum, green, and white coloring of the thyme create a striking setting near the long, flowing leaves of the grass. The wine-colored *Sempervivum*, which look like tiny many-petalled red roses, have multiplied fast and trail down the stone wall in a V-shaped formation.

The fountain grass and these other plants are located on a corner with a gravel path coming from both directions. After a half dozen years or so, the grass has gotten large, almost four feet wide. Soon I will divide it, since I do not want it to swallow up the other diminutive plants.

In addition to placing smaller plants near the fountain grasses, I have used large perennials, such as the five-foot-tall, late-summer-flowering *Solidago altissima* (goldenrod), with its showy chartreuse inflorescence. An excellent shrub to use as a backdrop to the grass and the goldenrod is *Ribes aureum* (golden currant). This drought-tolerant shrub, a common sight on the plains and in the foothills of Colorado, glows burgundy in fall next to the creamy-white flowers of the grass.

'Moudry' is a midsized variety of fountain grass. At just two feet high and wide, it is a jewel of a plant for small or large gardens. 'Moudry''s distinguishing feature is its deep purple flowers. I grew this plant for a few years, and then, wrongly thinking it needed to be divided, did so and killed it! I should have waited another year or two for it to get more robust. Truthfully, it had not gotten terribly large; I was just in a hurry. Once established, 'Moudry' self-sows at an alarming rate, especially in moist sites, so be watchful of overwatering this grass and cut off the flower stalks after you have enjoyed the color. In some years, the plant does not flower. Wondering about its flowering potential one late autumn day, I inspected the foliage in detail, and lo and behold, found tiny, dark-colored plumes that appeared itching to emerge. Alas, within days a

---

LEFT: *The pale beige seedheads of fountain grass* (Pennisetum alopecuroides) *cascade by the reddish greenery of black chokeberry* (Aronia melanocarpa).
RIGHT: *Occasionally fountain grass* (Pennisetum alopecuroides) *will not bloom. Here the greenery turns a brilliant burnt orange among the floating purple florets of* Verbena bonariensis.

frost arrived and no plumes appeared. Even if 'Moudry' does not flower, I treasure its golden yellow autumn sheen and balloonlike shape, which has a crease in the center, reminding me of a book parted in the middle.

In my experience, overall the pennisetums self-sow minimally and are easily managed, which make them practically perfect grasses for any size of garden.

Helictotrichon sempervirens (blue oat grass) rarely self-sows. Its needle-thin leaves rise up from a well-formed clump. It reaches over two feet high and tilts outward at the edges. When its light khaki-colored flowers shoot out neatly from its almost iridescent blue leaves in late spring, this increases its height approximately two feet. As summer kicks in, blue oat grass is in full swing, a neat symmetrical plant standing at attention, ready to be flanked by a rich tapestry of perennials.

Many perennials add flare to this grass. Artistically speaking, yellow and blue are two colors that favor each other's company. As the blue oat grass showers my garden with its bouffant headdress and sways gently in any wind, *Centaurea macrocephala* (yellow hardhead), a staunchly rigid perennial, is camouflaged in the background. Its

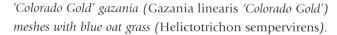

*'Colorado Gold' gazania (*Gazania linearis *'Colorado Gold')*
*meshes with blue oat grass (*Helictotrichon sempervirens*).*

long leaves are three inches wide and produce lollipop-sized yellow flowers that appear to drift behind the grass.

I have several blue oat grasses strategically placed around my garden. This is one of my most treasured grasses because it can be used in diverse ways. In one spot I planted the geranium 'Patricia', which is covered with volumes of pink flowers that look like pink polka dots and that are almost hidden behind the steely blue leaves of the grass. To further accent the blue foliage, in mid-spring blue spheres of *Allium caeruleum* syn. *A. azureum* (blue allium) are splashed across my landscape. Its round balls rise from two-foot-tall skinny stems and floppy thick leaves. Plant these in the vicinity of blue oat grass and I guarantee you'll enjoy the scenery! A quirky feature of this onion is that after a few years it will seed itself promiscuously around the garden, bringing in the welcome shade of blue. In late summer, the blue color of the onion fades and turns a stunning hue of ivory, which looks perfect around blue oat grass. For a different effect around the grass, try another ornamental onion, *Allium tubero-sum* (garlic chives). At eighteen inches high, its golf ball–sized white flowers bloom

---

*The bright flowers of coreopsis and trumpet lilies add emphasis to the towering leaves of blue oat grass (*Helictotrichon sempervirens*).*

LEFT: *The yellowish green foliage of lady's-mantle (*Alchemilla mollis*) spreads across the foreground of this picture, while blue oat grass (*Helictotrichon sempervirens*) dominates the background.*
RIGHT: *A red rose and the burgundy blossoms of* Coreopsis *'Limerock Ruby' snuggle between blue oat grass (*Helictotrichon sempervirens*) and the greenery of maiden grass (*Miscanthus sinensis *'Gracillimus').*

in clusters in late summer, a welcome sight that signals cooler weather is fast approaching.

I'm thrilled when I discover new plants; I purposely seek them out at nurseries. Recently I've become enamored with varieties of *Kniphofia* species (red-hot poker). Their vibrant colors and rocketlike appearance look spectacular scattered among blue oat grass, as well as near any silvery plants. They adapt to dry or average moisture conditions and come in various heights. Because of their loud colors of siren orange and blazing yellow, these long-blooming plants, which produce many flowers on a single plant, will draw attention wherever they are placed. Two excellent selections are *K.* 'Alcazar', with salmon-colored flowers, and *K.* 'Coralina', whose florets are coral-red.

A stately grass that is never hidden anywhere is *Saccharum ravennae* or *Erianthus ravennae* (hardy pampas grass). In a large garden, this fashionable grass dominates any space. Once the old stems are cut down in March, new growth arises within weeks on this upright clump-forming grass. By July, the grass is about half its potential size at five feet tall. During this stage, it has formed its grass "skirt," about two feet high, ringing the erect stems. The skirt, made up of many half-inch-wide green leaves, vaults upward, then billows down, curving to touch the surface below. Eventually the grass and its cottony flowers in silvery white to beige—which alone are a foot long—may reach

Fine hairs of blue oat grass (Helictotrichon sempervirens) *dance above the dark purple flowers of meadow sage* (Salvia nemerosa) *and 'Moonshine' yarrow* (Achillea 'Moonshine'), *while faces of trumpet lilies shout. (photo by Robert Bridges)*

The early-growing leaves of hardy pampas grass (Saccharum ravennae)
wind and dip through 'Marjorie Fair' rose.

twelve feet high and three to four feet across, depending on the amount of water the plant receives. Excessive moisture or rich soil will lead to loose growth. At this point, the grass may need to be stalked. Every five years or so hardy pampas grass is in need of maintenance. When the inside stems begin to deteriorate and appear dark brown, pampas grass is sending a clear signal to the gardener that division is necessary.

The utilitarian aspects of this grass are many. Because of its nearly treelike proportion, it can be practical and aesthetically pleasing as a screen or hedge, as a surround for patios, and to create a staging area for garden parties in late summer or fall or even in the rare warmish days of winter. My large specimen of hardy pampas grass is enveloped by tiny stone pebbles, purple asters, and the cloudy white flowers of *Boltonia asteroides* 'Snowbank' (Boltonia), along with an annual yellow daisy. Another innovative idea when using this statuesque grass is to mass low-growing annuals at its feet.

A plant that intrigued me as I searched for something special at the nursery was *Silphium laciniatum* (compass plant). The name and its daisy flowers enticed me, so I bought it instantly! Its copious yellow-cupped flowers appear on branching stalks, and its artichoke-green leaves are distinctly lobed, while the bottom leaves are hairy. Compass plant, native to portions of the Midwest, stands well alongside the imposing hardy pampas grass.

Pioneers of earlier centuries used compass plant stalks to mark the edges of wagon routes over the wild prairie. They tied scraps of cloth to these stalks to indicate where there were swales or other passages that might be difficult or dangerous, trying to ensure safe passage through the virgin lands for pioneers who followed. In addition, the pioneers discovered that the plant's sap produced a palatable form of chewing gum. Although I grow the compass plant, I have not tasted the sticky gum that comes off the upper third portion of the stem.

When a native prairie plant, such as the compass plant, originally from Kansas, Nebraska, or South Dakota, unites with the hardy pampas grass, which is native to

Hardy pampas grass (Saccharum ravennae) _shoots upward and plays off surrounding perennials, like white Boltonia_ (Boltonia asteroides 'Snowbank'), _purple asters, and an annual yellow daisy._

LEFT: *The detailed, ropelike plume of a single* Miscanthus *stem.*
RIGHT: *At Thanksgiving, maiden grass (*Miscanthus sinensis *'Gracillimus') displays russet color. Seedheads of black-eyed Susan (*Rudbeckia hirta*) frame the fine-textured foliage of tufted hair grass (*Deschampsia cespitosa*).*

northern Africa and the Mediterranean region, magic happens in terms of beauty, contrast, texture, and geography. This international collaboration becomes even more fascinating when I consider the fact that both plants are growing in an average garden in Littleton, Colorado!

Partners in Motion

Miscanthus is a highly respected genus of grasses to use in the home landscape. Native to eastern Asia, Africa, and Japan, these grasses flower when they receive sufficient moisture. They are not a dryland plant. Sometimes, because of lack of moisture, *Miscanthus* grasses do not flower, sending up only foliage, which also grows shorter with less moisture. Even without the flowers, however, *Miscanthus* creates a gorgeous effect with its shape and sheer volume of lines.

Miscanthus sinensis 'Yaku jima' adorns my garden as one of my early purchases in this grass genus. This name is used for several species, all found growing naturally on the Japanese island of Yakushima. 'Yaku jima' has been a consistent companion and performer for me for more than a decade. Like most grasses, it requires minimal care. In late winter or early spring 'Yaku jima' needs to be cut down to about twelve inches. The

*Backlit, maiden grass (*Miscanthus sinensis *'Gracillimus') exhibits its robust greenery.*
Purple tufts of Verbena bonariensis *and the yellow disks of black-eyed Susan*
*(*Rudbeckia hirta*) frame maiden grass. (photo by Robert Bridges)*

ABOVE LEFT: *A halo of ivory* Miscanthus sinensis *'Yaku jima'*
is queen of the garden as it showers above Verbena bonariensis.
ABOVE RIGHT: *In the midst of autumn, the sandy, draping leaves of* Miscanthus sinensis *'Yaku jima'*
contrast with the burgundy and green foliage of 'Ferdy' rose.
BELOW: *'Ferdy' rose blooms peachy-pink, while the stems of* Miscanthus sinensis *'Yaku jima' bend*
among assorted perennials, such as vertical salvias, bloody cranesbill ground cover,
*and the pincushion flowers of 'Pink Mist' scabiosa (*Scabiosa columbaria *'Pink Mist').*

previous year's cut plumes offer many possibilities, from holiday decorations, to compost, to mulch for flower beds. Once cut down, the bare stems feel like strong bristles.

In June, the plumage of 'Yaku jima' has grown to about two feet high and curves within itself like the letter C. Three plants placed in an easy-to-view location near a path dip in and out of numerous perennials and shrubs. Throughout most of my garden, the plants are close together, giving my garden a lush, full look. In addition, the plants work as a mulch and block out the sun, which inhibits weeds. I am careful not to plant so close that the feathery blooms of the grasses look crowded and are not able to expand well. Three or four feet between plants is a good distance for this grass. If the spirit moves me, I tuck in a few *Verbena bonariensis*, a tall reseeding annual with clusters of small round purple flowers at the tip. It casually braids itself into the puffy whitish flower heads of 'Yaku jima'. The species name, *bonariensis*, adds to the international flare of my garden, since *bonariensis* indicates where the plant was first discovered—in Buenos Aires in 1726.

My garden has a single specimen of *M. sinensis* 'Graziella'. I don't have many perennials around 'Graziella', which allows the viewer to see all its different parts.Its long thin stems, which contrast with the stout globular form of 'Yaku jima'. 'Graziella' stands out like a peacock, strutting its plumage and waiting to be admired. Various rudbeckias

---

LEFT: Verbena bonariensis *transforms to a leathery-brown color close to the bluish flowers of false sea holly (*Eryngium planum*) and the tan seedheads of* Miscanthus sinensis *'Yaku jima'.*
RIGHT: *The statuesque flowers of feather reed grass (*Calamagrostis acutiflora *'Karl Foerster')
flaunt their feathery tops near the fanciful flowers of* Miscanthus sinensis *'Yaku jima'.*
*The gray leaves of silver sage (*Artemisia cana*) and the pink blossoms of 'Max Frei' German soapwort
(*Saponaria lempergii *'Max Frei') add texture and color to the pageantry.*

complement the grass. Also nearby is a sweet-smelling five-foot-tall rose with many petals, 'Therese Bugnet', which repeat blooms (meaning to bloom more than once in a season). Throughout most of the year, the rose's canes are a glossy deep red. Blooming earlier in this area is *Papaver dubium* (long-headed poppy), with a reddish pink flower about the size of a half dollar, dotted green in the center. Topping off the scene, the fall leaves of the grass turn hues of burgundy, with a paler color running down the middle. At this time of year, the leaves remind me of ribbons I might use to wrap packages during the upcoming holiday season.

Since my garden is more than fifteen years old, many plants have begun to reseed, popping up in undesirable locations. Cleaning out small seedlings, such as the poppy and the verbena just mentioned, from among slender-thin blades of grass or when they are mixed in with perennials is tedious. I try to weed out these volunteers early in the season so they won't disrupt the growth of the grasses or crowd them out.

A large grass I've been growing for a number of years is *M. sinensis* 'Variegatus' (variegated Japanese silver grass). Pronounced stripes of creamy white and green color run up and down the length of the five-foot grass. Once mature, the foliage hangs down, giving

---

The amber-colored sprays of Miscanthus sinensis *'Graziella' loom above black-eyed Susan (*Rudbeckia hirta*).*

*Variegated Japanese silver grass (*Miscanthus sinensis *'Variegatus') huddles among spikes of speedwell (*Veronica spicata *'Blue Charm') and the furry flowers of joe-pye weed (*Eupatorium purpureum maculatum *'Gateway').*

this grass a graceful though triumphant image. A few of its leaves jut out in a random pattern into nearby plants, such as through *Eupatorium purpureum maculatum* 'Gateway' (joe-pye weed), with its large plum flowers and long pointed leaves. The five-inch-long, curly flowers of the grass emerge in September out of pinpoint-sharp sheaths and remain strong and lively through most of winter, unless a fierce storm pounds them to the ground. Blooms appear most years, unless moisture is insufficient or the plant needs to be divided. Unlike *M. sinensis* 'Yaku jima', which needs division every three or four years (and more often if planted in richer soils), *M. sinensis* 'Variegatus' goes without attention longer. After six years, my specimen is just more than two feet wide. Its bleached, winter stalks intertwine nicely with the canes of one of my precious shrub roses.

The common name of *M. sinensis* 'Strictus'—porcupine grass—led me to purchase this plant I now cherish. This decorative plant stands in a corner of my garden near a flagstone walkway and a smooth granite boulder. Its upright stems, with their vase-shaped habit, look like swords awkwardly pointing outward. On its leaves are creamy yellow horizontal stripes, alternating with jade green. Its typical fall flowers come in September and are bronze, but dry to a soft tan as snow and cold bite the garden. Over the years, it has remained five feet tall and barely three feet wide. It is crowded among a few perennials, and I suspect it might reach more than six feet in height and expand in width if given more space. Giving this grass and others more space will allow you to relish their full potential in flower, form, size, and color. Many perennials snuggle around porcupine grass. I have used *Heliopsis helianthoides* (false sunflower), with its cotton ball–sized yellow flowers; this plant stretches to about the same height as the grass. The grass and the sunflower lean into each other, an unruly garden style that I favor. In late summer and fall, *Eryngium planum* (false sea holly) adds a glimmering tint of blue to this site.

I have a few immature plants of *Miscanthus* that I know will put on growth in the coming years. I carried *M. sinensis* 'Adagio' in a small container from the East Coast, moving it carefully from plane to car and back again. While planting grasses in the fall is not recommended, it has worked for me. I do keep a watchful eye to make sure grasses don't dry out if I plant in the fall. Since I planted 'Adagio' quickly in the fall before the ground froze and the snow blew in, it's not ideally located. Until I move it, I'll gingerly step around other plants to admire the grass. The green stems of 'Adagio' are among the thinnest of all the *Miscanthus* grasses. Some of the five-foot-tall stems crisscross each other in a sweeping manner. This grass starts blooming in August with flowers that resemble those of *M. sinensis* 'Yaku jima'. The flowers have a slight reddish tint and the foliage turns yellow in fall. Complementing the yellow foliage is a trio of nearby *Rudbeckia nitida* 'Herbstsonne' syn. *R. nitida* 'Autumn Sun' (shining coneflower), a gigantic coneflower more than five feet tall. Its yellow ray florets have protruding green centers. This upright perennial, like all my grasses, never needs staking.

Two other *Miscanthus* grasses are in full view on the south side of my front garden. I've planted them in a checkerboard pattern: a rose, a grass, a rose, and a grass. As the grasses become larger, their long lanky stems will wind themselves among the mostly firm but bendable thorny canes of the shrub roses. *Miscanthus sinensis* 'Silberfeder' (silver feather maiden grass) will grow to about six feet and, beginning in August, will display silvery plumes with a touch of pink. Sometimes the habit of this grass can be limp, but that doesn't interfere with its beauty. To the contrary, this growth habit makes it a vivid companion next to the more rigid upright roses. The rose on one side is a *Rosa spinosissima* (Scotch rose), which blooms profusely one time in June with

*Purple love grass (*Eragrostis spectabilis*) is frothy in front of the symmetrical lines of feather reed grass (*Calamagrostis acutiflora *'Karl Foerster').*

single white-tinged pink blossoms that carry a light sweet scent. The pencil-thin stems of the rose are a mass of small sharp bristles. Next comes the silver feather grass, and in the center is the vase-shaped form of *Rosa* 'Charles de Mills', an old-fashioned rose that dates to before the 1700s. Its voluptuous highly fragrant flowers, which are purple and crimson, appear once for a few weeks in June. After its flowers fade, the plant's foliage acts as a backdrop to the grass and other perennials.

The final grass in this design quartet is *M. sinensis* 'Morning Light'. Its foliage is slender and when the grass blooms in late summer and fall, the top few inches shine a pleasing shade of pink. In cold regions like mine, I suspect this grass will not exceed four and a half feet in height.

I planted my shrub roses years ago when I wasn't familiar with the many varieties that repeat bloom. To add pizzazz to your garden, use repeat-blooming roses, which flower in fall, coinciding with the drama of the grasses. The taller Canadian roses are excellent choices, since they are hardy, disease-resistant, and drought-tolerant. 'John Cabot', with deep rose-pink semi-double flowers, grows to about six feet—or if a trellis is nearby, use the rose as a climber where it can reach ten or twelve feet in height. Another variety that makes a good companion to *M. sinensis* 'Silverfeder' is the six-foot-high and -wide rose 'Adelaide Hoodless'. Its double flowers bloom in July and again in September. Planted behind *M. sinensis* 'Morning Light', the red color of the rose and the pink plumes of the grass sparkle together in the sunlight.

A final rose to use in front of either grass is 'Henry Hudson'. Although small in stature, under two feet, the rose is effective when planted in pairs or a trio. Since I've grown this rose for a number of years, I can well imagine how three of them would look nestled near the base of any *Miscanthus* grass. The rose's fat, pink buds open to reveal double white flowers that are tinged pink and carry a light fragrance.

A grass that adds a dash of romance to the garden is *Eragrostis spectabilis* (purple love grass). Lest the gardener get too carried away with romantic thoughts, it is best to

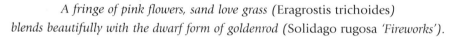

*A fringe of pink flowers, sand love grass (*Eragrostis trichoides)
*blends beautifully with the dwarf form of goldenrod (*Solidago rugosa 'Fireworks').

remember this grass easily self-sows. To limit this activity, cut off the seedheads soon after the grass has flowered and curtail the amount of water it receives. Even with this slight drawback, the charm of purple love grass transcends this small flaw. In fall, its copious flowers seem to gush like an oil well from the solid ground. The purplish pink hair-thin flowers open and then fall and bend on nearby plants and structures.

If your garden soil is sandy, infertile, or poorly drained, purple love grass is a perfect pick. Soothing to look at, a ribbon of this grass brings smiles when planted among dozens of native yellow daisies. If your area has been amended with a bit of compost, try the long-blooming perennial *Coreopsis* 'Limerock Ruby' (red tickseed), with deep maroon flowers. If you are in a region where temperatures dip to ten degrees below zero, mulch around this plant. Otherwise you'll lose it as I did!

Eragrostis trichoides (sand love grass) is a relative of purple love grass. Not as vigorous as its cousin, this two- to three-foot grass is one of my prized possessions. Its lackadaisical green foliage droops down one side. The flowering plant resembles water shooting straight out from a hose, as pinkish flowers squirt up to announce their presence. This picture becomes even more satisfying when the three-foot, bright yellow clustered blossoms of *Solidago rugosa* 'Fireworks' (goldenrod) cozy up to the grass. These two unique plants create a perfect combination.

Another grass I like to grow is *Stipa* (feather grass). A clump-former, this grass prefers good drainage and thrives in full sun. It also adapts to dry rocky slopes and dislikes heavy wet soils or shady sites. The flowers of feather grass are among the showiest in the ornamental grass kingdom, with delicate hairlike leaves.

Recently I purchased *S. capillata* (needle grass), which is native to parts of Europe and Asia. Since mine has only been in the ground for two years, it has not yet shown the plant's characteristic long sprays of silvery-white inflorescences that create a windswept sort of elegance. At three feet tall, my specimen can be seen easily from a few different angles. To spiff up the view in summer when the awns (bristles or spines at the tips of grass bracts) appear, I plan on planting hybrid penstemons like *Penstemon* 'Firebird', known for its red flowers, and *Penstemon* 'Prairie Dusk', which has purple flowers. Shrubs are also worthy plants to use among grasses because their woody branches add structure to the planting site. One that likes the same conditions as the penstemon and the *Stipa* is *Elaeagnus commutata* (silverberry). Although it is not widely available, this ten-foot-high shrub is worth finding because it has reddish brown branches and silvery-green curved leaves. The backs of the leaves have the bonus of an uncommon silvery sheen. These features add fine punctuation near the grass.

Now that I have been growing grasses for many years, they provide me with benefits in addition to their beauty. When I divide grasses in my garden, I bring the extra clumps to a local nursery, where the owner divides them into smaller bundles and sells them to plant-hungry customers. In exchange for the grasses, I get to pick and choose plants from his nursery—I feel like a hungry customer at a buffet! On one such trip, I considered *Juncus effusus* (common rush), which I admire for its uncommon spiral-like leaves, but I left it for fellow customers. Years ago, I killed a common rush by planting it in a dry location, not realizing it was happiest in water gardens or swampy habitats.

On this visit I chose *Spodiopogon sibericus* (Siberian graybeard or frost grass). In three or four years' time, the plant in my four-inch pot will swell into an elegant mushroom-shaped sphere with half-inch-wide, medium green foliage. The plant's fuzzy, nearly one-foot-long plumes, which bloom in July and August, are evenly distributed over the leaves. Once in flower, the grass is four feet high and wide. As the season progresses, the grass turns red, which allows it to blend well with other fall-blooming plants such as *Aster*, *Boltonia*, and *Rudbeckia*. At the onset of winter, when a hard frost zaps the garden, the entire plant is etched in a sheet of frost, which is why it is commonly called "frost grass."

The other plant that would have been a sweet choice, had it been stocked at the nursery, is *Sporobolus heterolepis* (prairie dropseed). Prairie dropseed brings movement and an immense range of color and texture to the garden. This is a bunchgrass, which prospers, albeit slowly. Give this grass at least four years to mature and show off its gallant display of plumage—in dry areas. Its refined plumes remind me of the arrows I played with as a child at summer camp. This long-lived and trouble-free plant succeeds in most soils, even heavy clay where there is poor drainage. Unlike most grasses, which age over time and often need division, this grass does not die out in its center and will last for decades without any renewal. Because of the plant's extremely dense root system, it *can* be divided, but the task would be daunting. Prairie dropseed has an unusual quality for a grass: fragrance. Some people describe the scent as sweet or pungent, while others are reminded of crushed cilantro or burnt popcorn. If your curiosity has been piqued, buy this grass and see what your nose decides!

Prairie dropseed offers varied foliage colors through the seasons. November foliage may be a bold orange, while the leaves in July look like thin threads of green. In early September, the plant's blooms carry silver accents. Because of the fine-spun nature of the flowers on prairie dropseed, they take a whipping when winds swoop down on the prairie. The same effect can be witnessed in the home garden during a high wind. If you see batches of prairie dropseed in its native prairie habitat, consider yourself fortunate. You have likely come face-to-face with undisturbed prairie. Extensive overgrazing and farming have eliminated many of these native plants, making them a rare sight indeed. To re-create the feel of the prairie, string together, alongside the grass, the brilliant yellow rays of any daisy plant. It has been said that because of the extensive amount of daisies that smother the prairie in fall, instead of being called "grassland" it should be called "daisyland."

Grasses That Adapt

Grasses have the ability to adapt to a wide range of conditions, such as sun, partial shade, heavy soils, and sandy soils. However, in a few cases it is beneficial to research the special needs of certain grasses to achieve the best results. It is helpful to be aware of soil conditions. *Schizachyrium scoparium* (little bluestem) will not thrive in heavy clay

---

An attractive accent when in flower and with lively foliage colors,
prairie dropseed (Sporobolus heterolepsis) will definitely appeal to a wide spectrum of gardeners,
especially when combined with the purple flowers of speedwell (Veronica oltensis)
and the leafy greenery of spurge (Euphorbia segueriana niciana).

soil; it requires good drainage to develop a proud show of its dashing golden-orange fall color.

In recent years, as I drive to a nearby college where I teach gardening, I have noticed long sweeps of little bluestem planted in a wavy pattern in front of a random group of tall pine trees. Growing across from a car dealership and in front of a stone wall, the clumps of burnt orange grass look playful, bouncing to and fro in the wind. Little bluestem brings a refreshing view to this average suburban neighborhood, providing a nice change from familiar mugho pine and juniper. I do like some junipers. However, when the same ones become ubiquitous in public landscapes, my eyes grow weary. Some landscapers are breaking from this habit, trying different plantings around malls and fast-food restaurants. In our dry climate in the Rockies, little bluestem and other grasses are not only gorgeous—they are practical!

As a companion to little bluestem, I have planted *Chamaebatiaria millefolium* (fernbush). This medium-sized shrub, which occasionally reaches five or six feet, is an ideal

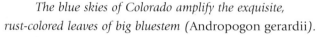

The blue skies of Colorado amplify the exquisite,
*rust-colored leaves of big bluestem (*Andropogon gerardii*).*

choice next to the grass. In summertime, it produces small white, delicately aromatic flowers and green-gray foliage, providing a smashing backdrop for the blue-green color of the grass. The leaves of the fernbush, which look like miniature ferns, are often ever-green in warmer regions or "eversilver." In winter, the twisted woody stems of the fernbush are an attractive counterpoint to the ravishing reddish color and soft moving lines of the grass. If you want to create a prairie setting with summer-into-fall appeal, plant the following wildflowers: *Asclepias tuberosa* (butterfly weed), *Ratibida columnifera* (Mexican hat), or various *Penstemon* varieties (beard tongue). Finally, in front of little bluestem and for an outstanding view in fall, I suggest *Marrubium rotundifolium* (round-leaved horehound), with its lime green, soft, and felted foliage. My horehound drapes over a short granite wall with little bluestem raised up a few inches behind it.

The horehound would also be appropriate along a wall or on the ground with *Andropogon gerardii* (big bluestem) in the background or a fair distance away. In close proximity to horehound, big bluestem would dwarf it, since the latter is under a foot tall in fall, compared to the five- to eight-foot height of big bluestem. This grass is most suitable for gardeners who have large plots of land; however, one or two of these grass plants would be a distinctive presence in a medium-sized garden or a dry shrub border. In August, this strictly clump-forming grass has foliage, which is green or blue-green with tri-part soft pink seedheads. As fall marches forward, the entire plant consistently transforms to tones of copper and orange, a striking contrast to Colorado's blue skies.

At a plant sale a while ago, I bought a new selection of big bluestem, called 'Mega Blue'. I planted the small specimen, then ignored it for a few years. Now it is more than a foot tall and I'm doting on it, and enjoying the touch of the smooth foliage. I admire its steely blue-green leaves, whose top five inches look like they were dipped in burgundy paint. Not as big as the species *Andropogon gerardii* (big bluestem), the plant will be five feet tall and two feet wide according to its tag. Because I don't entirely trust information on plant tags—plants are sometimes bigger or smaller than stated—I'm guessing this grass will grow to about four feet tall (based on the exposed dry and windy conditions in my backyard). Time will tell.

When planting a shrub border to accompany either variety of big bluestem, use *Chrysothamnus nauseosus* (rabbitbrush), which is adorned with yellow fall flowers, and *Caryopteris* × *clandonensis* 'Dark Knight' ('Dark Knight' bluebeard or blue mist spirea), which is smothered on its stems by strong bluish purple flowers. To accent the smooth, luminous lines of the grass, I like *Caragana maximowicziana* (Maximowicz peashrub). This three-foot shrub, native to China and Tibet, has stems covered with intensely sharp thorns.

If conditions in your garden are less than perfect, *Panicum virgatum* (switch grass) should be your grass of choice; although its look is sharp, its presence is gentle. Switch grass has eye-catching, airy panicles, which are often tinted pink when they first open. Foliage beneath the plumes ranges from thin, wiry, and loose to unusually broad with strong blue coloring. It does fine in dry sandy or moist soils and even in heavy, clotted clay! To grow their best, switch grasses need good air circulation and sunny, open sites. In addition, although adaptable and mostly drought-tolerant, they do need a bit of moisture from late summer into fall to produce their robust panicles, which vibrate substantially when gusts of wind come along. Switch grass does well in moist soils, but too much consistent moisture will cause the grass to become invasive. Colorado's climate is noted for its 300 days of sun, and the soils in many areas are composed of hard, persistent clay. In such conditions, switch grass is absolutely perfect. Switch grasses range from four to eight feet in height, depending on the variety and on growing conditions.

Because of its adaptability to various soils, as well as its capacity to live long, switch grass can be counted on as a plant with practically limitless utility in the garden. Use

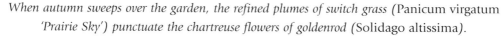

When autumn sweeps over the garden, the refined plumes of switch grass (Panicum virgatum *'Prairie Sky') punctuate the chartreuse flowers of goldenrod* (Solidago altissima).

*As the sun sets, the blue sky increases the outline of switch grass (*Panicum virgatum*).*

one as a focal point, or mass several together to create an artistic vignette, or arrange groupings of them to screen a patio from summer into fall. The grasses of this plant will tremble in summer breezes, then will shimmer in autumnal tones of golden yellow to shades of maroon.

From my perspective, the *Panicum* that has the strongest blue leaves is *P. virgatum* 'Dallas Blues'. In early summer, its ample foliage—leaves are almost an inch wide and narrow gradually, then bend downward toward the tips—is about two feet high and wide. This plant has even reached five feet in height in my garden. 'Dallas Blues' begins to produce its lavish plumage in late summer. Its foot-long flowers, which are brushed pale pink, measure almost four inches in circumference at the midsection. They feel light as a feather when touched from the bottom up. Autumn leaf color is tortoiseshell, changing to shades of coppery orange. 'Dallas Blues', like other switch grass, needs sufficient moisture from late summer into fall to create its floral display. To echo the pink coloring of the plumes of the grass, easy-to-grow, repeat-blooming shrub rose 'Flower

LEFT: *The horsetail-sized switch grass* (Panicum virgatum *'Dallas Blues'*)
is barely visible in back of 'Flower Girl' rose.
RIGHT: *A dusting of snow coats the garden, accenting fall color. 'Dallas Blues' switch grass*
(Panicum virgatum *'Dallas Blues'*) *is majestic among silver- and wheat-colored foliage plants.*

Girl' is a favorite companion. The semi-double pastel pink flowers with a dab of yellow in the center grow in large clusters. This rose is practically maintenance-free, a good trait for any plant, and one especially admirable in the rose world.

In contrast to the boldness of 'Dallas Blues', *P. virgatum* 'Heavy Metal' looks light and poetic, although its leaves are also blue. The foliage of 'Heavy Metal' is slender and stays under four feet. Its growth habit is strictly upright, unless plummeted by heavy snows. The plant's fine-textured panicles, which seem to sneak up on the plant in late summer, are tinted pale pink. 'Heavy Metal' rarely needs attention other than trimming off old foliage in early spring.

Switch grasses have long been appreciated in many European nations. As Americans are becoming more acquainted with grasses, more horticultural selections are available to the general public. I recently purchased *P. virgatum* 'Shenandoah', which will mature to three feet or taller. Its leaves are green in early summer, then slowly turn shades of deep red as cooler temperatures arrive. Star fall companions for 'Shenandoah' would be *Aster* and *Boltonia*, both daisies. Asters come in many colors, including pink, blue, and crimson. *Boltonia*, known for developing sturdy stems even without staking, yields vast numbers of snow-white, pink, or violet flowers, and is a long-lived perennial that only requires division every five to six years. In addition to these perennials, I like unusual annuals (as well as unusual perennials), those that catch your eye when you're visiting other people's gardens. I feel an affinity to passionate gardeners and can relate to what I recently read in a statement by garden writer Ken Druse. "If it's rare, we want it. If it's tiny and impossible to grow, we've got to have it. If it's brown, looks dead, and has black flowers, we'll kill for it."

In front of 'Shenandoah', I envision a dozen plants of *Salvia darcyi* (darcy sage). This shrubby annual has lipstick-red flowers that look like penstemon blossoms and extend a foot long. Its leaves are heart-shaped and sage scented. A big perk with this annual is that it tolerates light frost, so chilly fall temperatures don't signal an end to its performance. Because of this, it is a great partner for *Panicum*.

Two other selections of *Panicum* are *P. virgatum* 'Haense Herms' (red switch grass) and 'Red Cloud'. 'Haense Herms' tops out at less than four feet. Its frothy foliage, which is a mixture of red and green in late summer, turns predominately burgundy in autumn and dries to a light cappuccino color. I've seen this grass at large botanical gardens where its red fall foliage makes it a major attraction. 'Red Cloud' is a bit taller and also

---

*In summer, the thick, bluish green leaves of switch grass (*Panicum virgatum *'Dallas Blues'*)*
*curve down and join with the purple blossoms of blue allium (*Allium caeruleum*).*

*Several white coneflowers (*Echinacea purpurea *'White Swan') frame and contain the whispery, reddish seedheads of switch grass (*Panicum virgatum *'Rehbraun').*

strongly splashed with red. To spice up the straight lines of either grass, plant bunches of *Echinacea purpurea* 'White Swan' (coneflower). The white reflexed flower heads, punctuated with orange-brown disks, balance the thin lines of the grass. *Gaura lindheimeri* (whirling butterflies), with its specks of pink and white and willowy growth habit, is a worthy filler among the grasses.

Panicum virgatum 'Cloud Nine' stands far back in my garden, clearly visible from my office window. In late fall, after most of my perennials have turned to mush, this five-foot-tall switch grass stands robust like a tower. Its foot-long sandy-colored panicles, which are shaped like Christmas trees, rest gracefully on tawny and orange-colored leaves. A red and gray granite boulder highlights the airy fabric of the grass. In February or March, before doing major grass cleanup, I snip off the top foot of the floral beauty of 'Cloud Nine' to create a dried bouquet. I marvel at the plant's tiny teardrop seed-heads, with their black seeds tucked deep into the center. For thousands and thousands of years, along with the slow spread of underground roots, wind-dispersed seeds spread switch grass over the tallgrass prairie.

Spartina pectinata (prairie cord grass) is a rugged grass native to wetlands. This tough grass has been around for centuries as well. Prairie cord grass has extremely dense inter-locking roots; pioneers used it for floors and walls when they built sod houses. The wall of a sod house could be two feet thick, which kept summers cool and winters warm. However, according to John Madson, author of *Where the Sky Began*, leakage was often a problem! A woman from Nebraska with whom John Madson talked said her sod roof leaked a few days before a rain and several days after! Madson also discovered that to keep a dirt floor clean women would sprinkle salt on it and a tough crust would form that was almost like linoleum.

During a mild but cold winter, the windswept foliage of switch grass (Panicum virgatum) *looks blown away as it falls near a crushed stone path.*

Prairie cord grass has had various common names, including "ripgut" and "slough-grass." "Ripgut" speaks to its green leaf edge, which is finely serrated and sharp. Many early farmers, after suffering bloody hands, learned to use gloves when cutting this grass for hay. The common name "sloughgrass" arose because prairie cord grass is happiest in moist locations, or even submerged in water from one to six inches deep. Plant this grass in a pot first with heavy, loamy clay soil, and then plunge it in water. While prairie cord grass is considered an aquatic perennial great for water gardens, it will perform satisfactorily in a drier spot and can add excitement to a perennial border. In cold regions, prairie cord grass usually remains under three feet tall. Its stiff panicles, which bend slightly at their tips, appear in summer. At this time, the leaves take on a glistening golden-red sheen, which can be further highlighted when a few red and white water lilies float in a pond nearby. If possible, to really spiff up the picture, place the grass—three, four, or five of them—near any spruces covered with sharp, steel-blue needles.

Molinia (moor grass) also favors, but does not require, moist conditions. *M. caerulea* subsp. *arundinacea* 'Skyracer' (tall purple moor grass) was introduced in this country by Kurt Bluemel's nursery. The flowers appear like long bleached feathers on an arrow. After several years, my specimen has grown to three and a half feet in height. I suspect it may grow a few inches more, but probably not much more because of our dry climate. A clump-forming grass, its claim to fame—aside from the purplish tints—is the golden-yellow fall color of the leaves that some specimens have. Since the flower stalks are delicate, once a substantial snow hits, the entire plant collapses like a balloon with all its air let out. 'Skyracer', like other forms of tall purple moor grass, succeeds in most soils, including the alkaline soils common to the foothills of the Rockies. It will also succeed in partial shade.

I have planted asters close to 'Skyracer'. The woody characteristics and the odd forms of some shrub roses, along with their prickly thorns, make them congenial contrasts to the graceful texture of grasses. One selection I've used is 'William Booth', a hardy Canadian rose variety that spreads and trails but may grow to eight feet tall. This rose will survive and bloom well even when temperatures dip to thirty degrees below zero. Its unopened buds are deep red, and when the flowers are fully opened they are light red. This variety of rose is an especially good choice for 'Skyracer' because it will bloom repeatedly from June until September, when the grass looks good, too.

Carex (sedges) are grasslike plants from a large family of plants in which foliage, not flower power, is their best asset. Depending on how you divide them up, technically there are anywhere from 1,000 to 3,600 sedge species! Within these, colors span a

*The slight, golden foliage of tall purple moor grass (*Molinia caerulea *subsp.* arundinacea *'Skyracer')*
illuminates the circular flowers of a purple aster.

---

broad range and may be a shimmering green, tan, bronze, or yellow, or a combination
of those hues. Most sedges originate in habitats where the ground is moist to heavily
wet. However, in my experience, many adjust to drier soils. Some bask in sun; others are
successful in partial shade.

Carex muskingumensis (palm sedge) is native to wet woodsy areas in north-central
North America. Its name alone was a challenge for me to pronounce, but now it easily
rolls off my tongue! I saw this odd-looking grass that seemed tropical—hence its
common name—on one of my shopping sprees, and instantly placed it in my cart, not
thinking much about how it would grow or where. Since I did know that *Carex* liked
moisture, I planted it in a spot that receives water runoff and promptly ignored it for a
number of years. One day in June, as I weeded my garden, I noticed this grass had

formed an attractive large mass of light green foliage, which reminded me of a big balloon. Fed by the added moisture, the plant, traveling by underground rhizomes, had grown quickly to a height of two feet. The plant's top few inches are greenish tan flowers, not showy, but still adding graceful touches to the grass and the nearby plants.

From the one or two plants I had originally planted, many more accumulated in this area over time. I dug up a few clumps of this *Carex* and moved them to assorted places around my garden. I am very fond of this grass and the next time I divide it, I will plant it in a more conspicuous spot. Now it is placed at the edge of a prominent path, engulfed on all but one side by small pebbles. In late spring, *Iris lactea* (Mongolian iris), with its delightful pale purple flowers, blooms near the sedge. The grasslike foliage of the iris is a dull shade of pewter-blue green and its leaf is wider than that of the *Carex*, so the juxtaposition of these two plants is attractive. By late summer, the flowers on the *Carex* have faded, look bushy, and are colored a radiant honey tan, and its foliage is dry. I enjoy dipping my hand in the foliage and shaking the leaves, which produces a rustling sound.

*In spring, the bright green leaves of palm sedge (*Carex muskingumensis*) augment the lavender flowers of Mongolian iris (*Iris lactea*).*

*Around Halloween, palm sedge (*Carex muskingumensis*) has a bloom that resembles a fine-tipped paintbrush. The coppery-colored, grasslike plant is leather leaf sedge (*Carex buchananii*). Stonecrop (*Sedum 'Neon'*) completes the vignette.*

Where the ground receives little moisture and near a few red stones, I planted one clump of the palm sedge. It has grown to twelve inches, which shows how adaptable this grass is, and brings a nice mixture of green and tan to this hidden area.

Carex muskingumensis 'Oehme' (variegated palm sedge) has foliage that metamorphoses as the season progresses. The plant's leaves look as if a skilled painter has brushed yellow along the margins. I like this variegation in the garden, as long as it is not overdone. To complement the greenness of variegated palm sedge, I like to create contrast with the harsh pink flowers of *Tanacetum parthenium* 'Robinson Red' (painted daisy). In addition, the light pink and white flowers of cosmos weave through the grass, adding a casual look.

Don't be shy about planting unfamiliar grasses. Research them in advance, or take a chance and buy them on impulse. Either way, you will learn as they grow.

*A clump of blue fescue (*Festuca glauca*) chimes in well with various perennials like
the tinted blue flowers of sea holly (*Eryngium bourgatii*), yellow coreopsis,
and the big round star of Persia (*Allium christophii*).*

ABOVE LEFT: *Pink rose blossoms and an ornamental onion* (Allium caeruleum)
are intertwined with variegated Japanese silver grass (Miscanthus sinensis *'Variegatus').*
ABOVE RIGHT: *Blue oat grass* (Helictotrichon sempervirens) *squeezes close to the green leaves
of lady's-mantle* (Alchemilla mollis) *while a variety of coral bells hide in the corner.*
BELOW: *Blue oat grass* (Helictotrichon sempervirens)
partners up with black-eyed Susan.

ABOVE: *In autumn, a mound of mushroom-colored palm sedge* (Carex muskingumensis) *unites with rosy-cheeked stonecrop* (Sedum *'Neon').*

BELOW: *A quiet fall scene shows off greenery along with feather reed grass* (Calamagrostis acutiflora *'Karl Foerster'), an orange-flowered hyssop* (Agastache), *and far back a large mass of porcupine grass* (Miscanthus sinensis *'Strictus').*

ABOVE: *A wild panorama mixes the yellow foliage of giant reed* (Arundo donax) *with the expanded, soft flowers of Korean feather reed grass* (Calamagrostis brachytricha).
BELOW LEFT: *Dozens of spring-blooming dwarf bulbs* (Tulipa batalinii *'Bright Gem'*) *shine near the uncut wintry foliage of pony tail grass* (Nassella tenuissima).
BELOW RIGHT: *In a shady site, the seedheads of weeping sedge* (Carex pendula) *bend among the white flowers of* Corydalis ochroleuca.

ABOVE: *Weeping sedge* (Carex pendula) *is accentuated next to the purplish spring leaves
of purple smoke tree* (Cotinus coggygria).

BELOW: *The swaying plumes of blue oat grass* (Helictotrichon sempervirens), *along with a myriad of
perennials, create a festive occasion in summertime. Other plants in the picture: lady's-mantle*
(Alchemilla mollis), *meadow sage* (Salvia nemerosa), *spires of coral bells* (Heuchera sp.),
clematis (Clematis 'Proteus'), *deep pink blossoms of rose 'Morden Ruby'.*

ABOVE LEFT: *Often, but not always, an ornamental grass such as switch grass* (Panicum virgatum *'Prairie Sky') is not visually appealing when planted alone.*
ABOVE RIGHT: Miscanthus sinensis *'Variegatus' tightly bonds with joe-pye weed* (Eupatorium maculatum *'Gateway').*
BELOW: *Asters and 'Autumn Joy' stonecrop* (Sedum spectabile *'Autumn Joy')* *bump up the vertical lines of blue oat grass* (Helictotrichon sempervirens).

ABOVE: *Along with granite, stepping-stones, and the trailing blue spruce* (Picea pungens glauca procumbens), *the coppery lines of New Zealand hair sedge* (Carex comans) *enrich the splendor of this scene. The yellow flower is a shrubby form of strawflower* (Helichrysum splendidum).

BELOW LEFT: *Red switch grass* (Panicum virgatum *'Haense Herms'*) *is among the best selections for powerful burgundy foliage color in autumn.*

BELOW RIGHT: *As the weather chills, the sandy plumes of blue fescue* (Festuca glauca) *intermingle with two silver-leafed sages, the deep burgundy blooms of a sedum, and the yellow-tipped flowers of broomweed* (Gutierrezia sarothrae).

ABOVE: *Sneezeweed (Helenium sp.) leans on feather reed grass*
(Calamagrostis acutiflora 'Karl Foerster').
BELOW: *Ornamental grasses, along with other shrubs*
and perennials, sparkle in the fall sunlight.

CHAPTER THREE

Grasses and Their Shady Companions

Although many ornamental grasses thrive in the sun, gardeners blessed with shade should not be discouraged. There are many grasses that add serenity, color, and flair to the woodland garden, sheltered areas under trees, and other environments with limited sun. Grasses' graceful lines add variety to and complete the look of a perennial and annual garden.

My shade garden is dominated by a multistemmed cottonwood that has endured for more than twenty-five years. Beneath it are hundreds of

The two-toned green and tan flowers along the stems of Berkeley sedge (Carex tumulicola) are eye-catching in a mostly shade situation. They mingle well near the leaves of Christmas rose (Helleborus sp.).

perennials, bulbs, and ornamental grasses. On sun-drenched early spring days, before the cottonwood has leafed out, the blooms of colorful bulbs light up the landscape, pushing back winter. The brown soil cracks and heaves as plump yellow and purple crocuses and a swath of *Puschkinia scilloides libanotica* (striped squill), a bulb that dates from the early nineteenth century, force their way into the sunlight. The striped squill, about four inches high, is dotted with bell-like fragrant flowers. Narrow light blue stripes appear to be painted on the plant's white flowers. Complementing this sea of white is the uncommon *Ophiopogon planiscapus* 'Nigrescens' (black mondo grass).

In spring, the leaves of the one-foot-tall black mondo grass are blackish green and feel rough to the hands, especially toward their pointed tips. Unless winds are ferocious, the grass's bending stems remain somewhat immobile. As summer approaches, its foliage turns deep purple—in some lights it appears almost coal black. For a few weeks in summer, scant flowers show that are small and wine-colored. Once the blooms have faded, tiny spherical bluish black fruits add an intriguing look. Black mondo grass

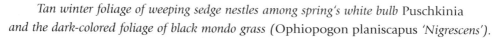

Tan winter foliage of weeping sedge nestles among spring's white bulb Puschkinia *and the dark-colored foliage of black mondo grass* (Ophiopogon planiscapus *'Nigrescens').*

*Black mondo grass (*Ophiopogon planiscapus 'Nigrescens'*) is subtle but showy near an assortment of ferns.*

spreads slowly. Eventually, I look forward to a large patch of it, nestled near the trunk of the cottonwood, since purple or blackish plants are especially wonderful for their special coloring. *Aruncus dioicus* (goat's beard) is a wonderful companion plant in this sea of dark foliage. Its creamy white panicles make a vibrant summer backdrop to the lower-growing black mondo grass. As an added bonus, the four- to six-foot goat's beard rarely needs dividing.

After the bulbs have had their heyday, two other plants usher in more zest in terms of color and appeal under this gigantic tree. *Bergenia cordifolia* (heartleaf bergenia) has thickish rounded leaves and grows to about a foot. Most varieties have maroon foliage, but the leaves of this variety, 'Bressingham Ruby', are deep red. In spring, its pink flowers stand out bravely next to the black mondo grass.

Carex pendula (weeping sedge) hovers above many of my perennials and bulbs. This sedge has long, taupe-colored flowers that hang down like thin whips. In moist locations, this three-foot grass spreads quickly; however, if seedlings are removed when the grass is just a few inches high, it is easily controlled. Keeping it drier is another method to stunt its wanderings. Don't be scared away by so-called aggressive grasses. Do not overwater them and many will provide breathtaking scenery.

Grasses in a woodland setting offer diversity against the architectural forms of tree trunks and their branches. The trunks are solid, some thick and some thinner. The bark on my cottonwood has many indentations and looks old. Sometimes I'll reach in with my hands, stepping carefully among the many plants beneath the tree, and feel, in a few spots, the corky texture of the tree. Each of the four trunks of my cottonwood measures almost a foot and a half across! At the base they look like giant spears shooting out of the ground.

Because the cottonwood is huge, sedges, other grasses, and perennials appear dwarfed by comparison, adding strong contrast beneath the bulky tree. Some grasses shake or quiver with a bit of wind, while others are tiny or so protected near the cottonwood that they barely move at all. One small sedge that stays more or less motionless is *Carex conica* 'Marginata' (Hime kan suge), also known as *C. conica* 'Snowline'. *Suge* is Japanese for sedge. My research states that this sedge may be slow to mature, which doesn't bother me since it is such a darling clump of wispy, variegated foliage. As I walk down my front steps to a few round paving stones that mimic real wood, I see the grass immediately. Two of these stones are spread sufficiently apart so that the grass fits comfortably, but snugly where I've planted it between them, looking secure and content. Although it has been in just one winter, I'm confident it will be long-lived, based on my years of success in growing sedges. Currently this one is four inches tall. Eventually, if it does rise to its potential of fifteen inches, I will move it to another location, equally visible.

A *Carex* that is planted in a perfect spot is *C. flacca* 'Burton's Blue'. This grass has many six-inch-long cylindrical stems, which stretch out from the center of the plant. The quarter-inch-wide metallic blue-green leaves add a few inches to its height, which overall is eight inches. Its tiny beige flowers are insignificant. The entire plant is attractive when the stems and the leaves rise up, fall down, and glide along the ground, reminding me of a slithering snake. A top-notch and easy geranium to grow near the *Carex* is *Geranium sessiliflorum* 'Nigrescens' (chocolate geranium). I let this geranium emerge

Although its flowers are insignificant, 'Burton's Blue' sedge (Carex flacca 'Burton's Blue') catches my eye because of the dull green coloration of its leaves.

---

wherever it pleases. The geranium looks like mini–mountain ranges that are four inches high scattered around the *Carex*. The chocolate-brown foliage of the geranium, with its intricate markings, complements the slender leaves of the *Carex*. In summer, this geranium produces small, button-sized whitish gray flowers that add special appeal.

Carex tumulicola (Berkeley sedge) is an excellent choice for shade, and in particular dry shade. Its lush, green, slender foliage with greenish tan seedheads that appear in late spring is stellar. The center of the sedge is somewhat empty and its dense leafage opens up and spreads out wide from that point. Overall, this sedge is a foot tall and fans out more than two feet. Since this grass adapts to dry shade, mine is planted near the foundation of my house, not far from my cottonwood tree, where moisture is kept to a minimum. Once established, the sedge is drought-tolerant. This grasslike plant will also thrive in a sunny location with average moisture. An ideal ground cover partner is any form of Christmas and Lenten roses (*Helleborus*). The handlike, bold leaves of this

Shiny miniature peppers sparkle as the sawlike foliage of northern sea oats
(Chasmanthium latifolium) *sways close by.*

handsome, easy-to-grow perennial contrast with the narrow foliage of the sedge. Like many grasses, this sedge is outstanding when several are grouped together.

A grass that deserves more attention is *Chasmanthium latifolium* (northern sea oats). Northern sea oats is native to wooded areas, mostly on the East Coast, although it can be seen in Texas in moist thickets. It is not fussy about its soil, adapting to a wide range of conditions, with the exception of heavy clay. Northern sea oats is at home in partially shaded areas with average to high moisture. It is a winner in dry shade; however, it grows at a slower rate, thus taking a longer time to produce its superior flowers.

Of all the grasses I grow, northern sea oats is high on my list because of its summer-blooming flowers. The light green flower becomes coppery in fall, and then changes again to a coffee color. About two inches high, the grass's cellophane-thin plumes, of which there are many, attach to slender stems. The thin plumes remind me of a two-sided saw since each floret, which is suspended downward, is neatly designed to look like teeth on a saw. The florets dance about vigorously whenever gusts of wind come along.

Unless the area is very moist, the plant limits its growth to three feet on average. Extra moisture will cause northern sea oats to spring up around the garden. Luckily for gardeners favored with moist soils, these young seedlings can be removed effortlessly with a simple hack of a weeding tool.

There are many partners for this grass. I recommend *Astilbe* (false spiraea) for its various summer-blooming color forms and its fernlike leaves. False spiraea, with its peacocklike plumes, looks best when a few are grouped together; these plants do require a moist location. For bronze foliage and dark red blossoms, seek out *Astilbe* 'Red Glow', just under two feet tall. If your location is dry, I champion hardy geraniums. A handsome plant, there is a wide selection from which to choose. Many have deeply divided leaves, and they appreciate light shade and dry to average moisture. But there are varieties that

---

*The yellow-green leaves of variegated Japanese sedge (*Carex morrowii 'Variegata'*) lighten up a shady site near the smooth leaves of heartleaf bergenia (*Bergenia cordifolia*) and the mottled foliage of cranesbill (*Geranium renardii*).*

As leaves drop, the sun filters through the plumes of bottlebrush grass (Hystrix patula).

work well in full sun. Hardy geraniums are useful as low ground covers, creating lovely contrast near the straight-up leaves and taller lines of the northern sea oats. *Geranium renardii* is planted throughout my garden. Nearly a foot tall, it has sage-green wrinkled leaves that feel springy when rubbed between one's fingers. Its pearly gray flowers are veined violet. Another geranium to team with any one- to two-foot grass is *G. sanguineum* (bloody cranesbill). About six inches tall, bloody cranesbill is not too finicky about dry or moist soils. Only very heavy clay soils and boggy conditions should be avoided. It spreads by underground roots and covers the ground to the edge of northern sea oats. Its cupped flowers are deep purple to crimson. The common name, bloody cranesbill, may relate to its red flowers; fall foliage is a patchwork of reds, greens, and bronze tones, ideal adjacent to the coppery hanging flowers of northern sea oats.

Northern sea oats may be tops in my garden, but *Hystrix patula* (bottlebrush grass), at two feet high, is dear to me for a number of reasons. First, I am originally from the eastern part of the country and this grass is native to that region, giving me a sentimental attachment. Second, I like its quirky botanical name because when in bloom, the six-inch-tall tawny flower head truly looks like a bottlebrush, an item that was useful in pre-dishwasher generations to scrub out baby bottles.

The distinctive flowering panicles on bottlebrush grass look best when three or more plants are grouped together; a single specimen may be easily overlooked. This grass responds well to dry shade and adapts to moister locations. If your bottlebrush is in dry shade, a companion plant amenable to those conditions and also tolerant of moderate periods of drought is *Euonymus fortunei radicans* 'Harlequin' (Japanese euonymus). My plant is young, but in a number of years this evergreen ground cover, with its exquisite green, cream, pink, and yellow speckled foliage, will mill around the feet of the bottlebrush.

Another woodland grass stamped with an odd botanical name is *Luzula sylvatica* (greater woodrush). A durable ground cover, it is ideal for difficult sites or erosion

---

*The leafy, biscuit-colored seedheads of woodrush (*Luzula sylvatica*) add diversity near dead nettle (*Lamium maculatum *'White Nancy'*). Hairy loosestrife (*Lysimachia ciliata*) and the mass of white flowers in the far left round out the panorama.*

control. Greater woodrush grows to a foot in height, with tiny, bell-like maroon flow-ers gathered in clusters on top of the foliage that bloom in spring. Its olive-green leaves are a half-inch wide and have curly off-white hairs along the margins. I have read that greater woodrush is vigorous, but I have not found that to be the case, perhaps because I hold back on watering.

A sturdy, easy-to-grow ground cover that I have used to encircle many grasses throughout my shady area is *Lamium maculatum* 'White Nancy' (dead nettle). Dead nettle is capped with smart-looking white flowers in spring, and its patchy green and white leaves last for years under average garden conditions. If you are looking for a more unusual plant, I suggest *Antheriscus sylvestris* 'Ravenswing' (cow parsley 'Ravenswing'). The plant's ravishing foliage is deep purple and its leaves have a fernlike pixie quality. The plant's stems are stout, which allows it to endure winds. Its lacy white flowers appear in clusters continuously from late spring into summer. The gorgeous 'Ravenswing' flowers and unusual foliage do well in full sun or light shade. 'Ravenswing' creates a festive scene among larger foliage plants or those with distinctive straight lines, such as grasses. My plant is near the weeping sedge, whose foliage is coarser and thick. From research and talking with colleagues, I learned that 'Ravenswing' will seed itself around, a fact I was delighted to hear.

To bring more color into a shady scene, plant *Brunnera macrophylla* 'Jack Frost' (Siberian forget-me-not). Adorned with puffy bright blue flowers, 'Jack Frost' also has prominent variegation on its heart-shaped leaves. If you are unable to find 'Jack Frost', buy the straight species. Either way, you will have groupings of white and bright blue flowers that will truly bring gaiety to a darkish corner of your garden. These are not low-water plants; they need medium moisture throughout the growing season.

I will never grow weary of *Deschampsia cespitosa* (tufted hair grass). In either full sun or light shade, tufted hair grass is a sturdy survivor. I appreciate its well-balanced dark green foliage and its translucent beige flowers. On a mountain hike in years past, I spot-ted a wide patch of tufted hair grass in a woodland setting. Dozens of unyielding aspen trees with their opaque bark and cylindrical trunks seemed to stand guard over the profuse, fluttery inflorescence of the grass below them. In my garden, the plant's silk-like downy green leaves are tucked tightly near the base of my roughly textured cottonwood. Here the grass receives a few hours of morning sun, after which it is shrouded in the shade of the cottonwood. Sprouting close by the grass are many other perennials. I grow *Asarum europaeum* (European wild ginger), a European native, with deep kidney-shaped glossy green leaves that grow close to the ground. In some climates,

*On the far left, variegated creeping soft grass (*Holcus mollis *'Variegatus') is caressed by the copious leaves of hosta (*Hosta sieboldiana *'Frances Williams'). Overlapping the hosta is the greenery of goat's beard (*Aruncus dioicus*).*

European wild ginger is evergreen, although this is rare for me. Springtime is supposed to bring greenish to purple flowers; my eyes have never seen this. Perhaps the ginger needs more water or higher humidity. Whatever it desires, it is not getting it in my garden. However, I still cherish it because I like how the round shiny leaves play off the slim leaves of the tufted hair grass.

A genuinely unusual grass for shade is *Holcus mollis* 'Variegatus' (variegated creeping soft grass). Under six inches and flowering rarely, the grass has green and white leaves that seem precisely painted by a fine-textured brush. Over the last eight years, creeping soft grass has spread so slowly across the ground in my garden that it is just a few inches wider than when I initially planted it. For this reason, I recommend that you avoid

LEFT: *Circular pink phlox softens the variegated lines of bulbous oat grass*
(Arrhenatherum elatius subsp. bulbosum*).*
RIGHT: *Hakone grass (*Hakonechloa macra *'Aureola')*
dips gently onto a slab of slate.

buying *H. mollis* (creeping soft grass). This green-leaved species, because of its naturalizing abilities, would quickly take over spacious areas.

Not invasive at all, at least not on the Great Plains, are hostas. I have only one, *Hosta sieboldiana* 'Frances Williams', a fine variegated form. Generally hostas are happiest in areas with more moisture. They are large and lush on the East or West Coast, where moisture is more abundant. But for gardeners in the interior West, I prefer and recommend euphorbia because it is easy to grow, likes average moisture, and has very appealing floral heads. The plant's decorative thin leaves are palmlike, appearing in irregular layers, and come in many attractive colors such as yellow, shades of green, and burgundy. Near my creeping soft grass, I grow *Euphorbia amygdaloides* 'Purpurea' (spurge). The russet foliage of the spurge adds elegance to the ground cover grass. It will reach more than two feet, decorated on top by stunning lime-green florets.

If you'd like a clump-forming grass with neater and more uniform leaves than the creeping soft grass, purchase *Arrhenatherum elatius* subsp. *bulbosum* 'Variegatum' (bulbous oat grass). The plant's low-growing greenery, about a foot tall, appears from the base in late May and June. Where the grass receives too much sunlight and heat, it will sulk and look a bit ratty. But once cool weather arrives and the plant's brownish foliage is snipped off, its leaves will give an encore performance and shine on into fall. This grass produces unusual, pearl-sized, rootlike parts at the base of the stems, which are visible when one wants to divide or move the grass. To keep this grass fresh-looking, division every two or three years is recommended.

A single specimen of bulbous oat grass works well in any high-traffic area, where all who walk by can take notice. Because it has light-colored leaves, bulbous oat grass is striking near any red-colored stone. If you have the space, plant a dozen or so grasses a few inches apart near a patio to create a screen or at the edge of a woodland area with trees in the background. Adjacent to any of these areas, in a sunny spot, try another euphorbia. I have a real fondness for *E. amygdaloides* 'Rubra' (red wood spurge). The plant's florets have a spiral look, and their deep green shade creates a nice counterpoint to the bulbous oat grass.

A final grass that I've grown (and killed, several times) is *Hakonechloa macra* 'Aureola' (Hakone grass or golden Japanese forest grass). This grass is native to mountain ranges in Japan, more specifically to the island of Honshu and near Mt. Hakone, hence its common name. There are several varieties of Hakone grass. Although lovely, they require exact conditions to thrive—moist, well-drained soils, with adequate organic matter. In addition, they should be planted in a slightly protected spot—such as against a wall, close to a tree, or perhaps on the north side of the house. I have found them fussy, but other gardeners in the Denver area have grown them successfully. They will grow to about a foot, and their bending motion, plus their thin leaves and refined flowers, makes them appealing to gardeners looking for a unique planting in a shady spot. Variegation is also a big draw for gardeners. So even though this grass is somewhat difficult to grow, there is a market for it in the Rocky Mountain region.

Although it is more challenging to find grasses suited to low-light areas than to full-sun areas, it is by no means an impossible task. While an average shade-tolerant perennial might struggle or need more care in a low-light area, the "right" grass will fit perfectly in a cooler and darker niche of the garden.

CHAPTER FOUR

Grasses as Ground Covers

Ornamental grasses are excellent as ground covers. Varieties exist for hot and dry locations, as well as for moist spots. Plant one or two grasses together or plant them in sweeps (meaning five or ten), making an oasis for the eyes. *Ground cover* is a flexible term. Grasses as ground covers need not remain only six inches in height or under. Be creative with your design ideas; try taller grass forms and mass them together.

Swirls of Blue Fescue

Common *Festuca glauca* (blue fescue) is a reliable grass that endures tough

---

In addition to its vivid, pink color in summer, 'Pink Crystals' ruby grass (Rhynchelytrum nerviglume) *metamorphoses to a nutshell brown. (photo by Robert Heapes)*

*Needlelike leaves produce graceful flowers on blue fescue (*Festuca glauca*).*
A low stone wall and annual larkspur complete the scene.

Colorado weather conditions with grace. Just provide full sun, and blue fescue will perform beautifully for years. This grass tends to self-sow after a few years, but not so prolifically that it becomes troublesome. If I'm not satisfied with where the fescue has settled on its own, I simply move it.

Fescues are dense clump-forming plants. They come in a myriad of blue tones with hues running the gamut of silver, gray, and shades of green. Their plumes, which light up the garden in autumn, are ivory, tan, or sometimes grayish or blue-green. Fescues vary in height from six inches to three feet, with most in the range of ten to fifteen inches, often taller in fall when they bloom. Modest in size, they adapt to diverse locations in the garden. One effective use of this small-statured grass is to plant it in drifts along the edges of a perennial border. In a rock garden arrangement, fescue's slender lines create a well-marked statement above a pool of pea gravel. The fescues also stand out well when arranged among other smaller plants such as veronicas (speedwell) and dianthus (pinks).

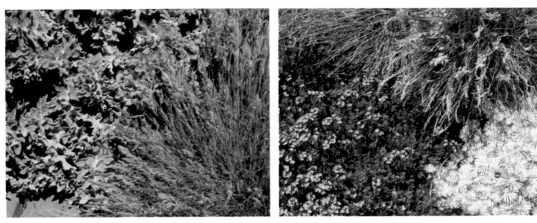

ABOVE LEFT: *Although lacking in bright colors, the rippled leaves of horned poppy* (Glaucium flavum)*, along with its gray-blue tint, are an ideal match near the red stone and thin leaves of blue fescue* (Festuca glauca)*.*

ABOVE RIGHT: *From above, blue fescue* (Festuca glauca) *helps frame the pink pinwheels of 'Mesa Verde' iceplant* (Delosperma kelaidis 'Mesa Verde')*, while the blue flowers of speedwell* (Veronica sp.) *hug the corner.*

BELOW: *A touch of tan with blue fescue* (Festuca glauca) *and variously sized stones unite the orange flowers of butterfly weed* (Asclepias tuberosa)*, the mat of partridge feather* (Tanacetum densum amanii)*, and the cottony seedheads of* Anemone multifida.

LEFT: *The cupped red flowers of cactus (*Opuntia polyacantha *var.* juniperina) *are dramatic as the hair-thin greenery of blue fescue (*Festuca glauca) *intertwines with the cactus pads.*
RIGHT: *Poppy mallow (*Callirhoe involucrata) *encircles a vibrant, blue-toned clump of blue fescue (*Festuca glauca).

While the fescues are not high-maintenance plants, they do benefit from some care to keep them fresh and tidy. When bunches no longer look vibrant or have grown too large for a location, simply divide them. I learned this easy solution from a gardening friend. A few years back, in late winter I saw a beautiful sweep of fescue at this friend's house. Placed near the low gray foliage of *Thymus pseudolanuginosus* (woolly thyme) and the upward-thrusting form of three dwarf evergreens, the fescue bunches provided short spurts of bright ocean blue, the antithesis of the evergreen and the matted thyme. I asked what extra work was involved for the grasses to look so perky, and she offered her simple maintenance solution. I had this exact plant at home, so, upon entering my garden that afternoon, I promptly grabbed my trowel, headed to my backyard, and began dividing my tattered and brown fescue. Since most of my fescues were planted many years ago, I had to tug and rip at the tufts to separate the dense root systems. Once replanted, the fescue rewarded me with glorious fountains of blue the following spring.

'Sea Urchin', 'Elijah Blue', and 'Boulder Blue' are fescue varieties that offer an even more intense blue than that of common blue fescue. Unfortunately, cultivars are often mislabeled and may be grouped as 'blue fescue'. Check out the plant carefully, or talk with knowledgeable nursery people to purchase, if possible, exactly what you want. No matter which cultivar you choose, fescues need well-drained soil, a bit on the dry side—no soggy feet for them.

When blooming, many grasses, including blue fescue, are semitransparent. As grasses bloom, the upper third of the grass begins to expand outward, creating a fan-shaped form. Even on the small scale of common blue fescue, this design element is effective. For example, a dianthus strategically placed behind the grass shows the fan shape to advantage. Although the majority of dianthus bloom in spring, *Dianthus nardi-formis* erupts in late summer with quarter-sized, pinkish lavender flowers above its cushion-forming mound of lacy, gray-green foliage. The small, dish-shaped flowers peeking through the thinly veiled blue foliage of the grass create a striking picture. Snaking between these two plants is *Callirhoe involucrata* (poppy mallow or wine cups). This ground cover has reddish purple flowers that bloom on and off from spring into fall. The plant's intricately shaped leaves also contribute a dash of the exotic.

Amber Waves

I grow *Carex comans* (New Zealand hair sedge) in a sunny, well-drained spot at the base of one of my rock gardens where water trickles down and moistens the soil. Because of

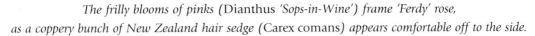

*The frilly blooms of pinks (*Dianthus *'Sops-in-Wine') frame 'Ferdy' rose,
as a coppery bunch of New Zealand hair sedge (*Carex comans*) appears comfortable off to the side.*

'Max Frei' German soapwort (Saponaria lempergii *'Max Frei') roams between purple coneflower* (Echinacea purpurea) *and the mopped head of New Zealand hair sedge* (Carex comans).

the moisture in this particular place, dozens of these sedges have emerged. New Zealand hair sedge varies in color: sometimes its weeping foliage is iridescent light green, while other times it is bronzier. I'm excited when I see pools of copper color, which circulate among the hundreds of small, glazed stones. When New Zealand hair sedge is young, the coppery-red and tan growth is just a few inches tall. As the plant matures, the length of the fine-textured leaves can stretch from six to eighteen or more inches. The grass forms an orderly clump; its flowing leaves rise a few inches, then abruptly bend downward and rest on the stones, creating a peaceful scene. I find the subtle, inch-long cylindrical flowers, a bit darker than gingerroot, appealing when they bloom each summer.

Since my garden is home to so many grasses, I sometimes forget to cut this one down, especially since it's so low to begin with. However, cutting it to within three or four inches of the ground in late winter or early spring is a good idea to keep its bronzy sheen polished and radiant-looking.

Closely related to the New Zealand hair sedge is *Carex buchananii* (leather leaf sedge). Much more erect than the New Zealand hair sedge, leather leaf sedge reaches more than two feet in height. Its leaves, as thin as violin strings, curve outward at the tips. The plant's flashy color is a mixture of amber, granite red, and ivory. I like to combine leather leaf sedge with various sedums. *Sedum spectabile* 'Neon', topped with brilliant candy-pink flowers, has scoop-shaped fleshy foliage that provides variation against the narrow leaves of the sedge. The lime-green color of the leaves also adds contrast near the coppery leather leaf sedge. The silver leaves of *Tanacetum densum amanii* (partridge feather), known for its pancake habit, would make another excellent selection in the vicinity of the sedge. However, since the partridge feather likes dry conditions, keep it a fair distance from the sedge.

Carex bergrenii (caramel carpet sedge) is a moisture-loving sedge that grows to barely four inches. I've squeezed this slow-spreading sedge between two stones where shallow puddles of water sometimes gather but then drain quickly. These are ideal

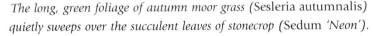

*The long, green foliage of autumn moor grass (*Sesleria autumnalis*)
quietly sweeps over the succulent leaves of stonecrop (*Sedum 'Neon'*).*

conditions for the sedge. The plant's brassy leaves look pleasing near the low-growing shrub *Salix arenaria* (creeping willow or blue creek willow) that is planted across the path. This willow, which also is fond of moisture, has a silvery velvet appearance from spring to fall. A dense shrub, reaching roughly two feet tall and wide, creeping willow is happiest in full sun, but light shade works too.

June Is Busting Out All Over

Stipa comata (needle-and-thread grass) is a fairly erect grass that reaches fifteen inches and adapts to moist or dry soils. It grows naturally on the open prairie in the mid-Atlantic states as well as in the intermountain region. While needle-and-thread grass does not stand out among the approximately 150 grasses in the tallgrass prairie, in my home

---

The dramatic size of colewort (Crambe cordifolia) *is a visual delight near the windblown display of needle-and-thread grass* (Stipa comata) *and the vertical blooms of clary sage* (Salvia sclarea).

LEFT: *In spring, hardy yellow iceplant (*Delosperma nubigenum*) drifts over a concrete edge, as pony tail grass (*Nassella tenuissima*) rises in the background.*
RIGHT: *In the midst of winter, the snow bends slender pony tail grass (*Nassella tenuissima*).*

garden it receives high marks. I have planted this grass in the middle of a raised berm that is about four feet high. Here the six-inch-long, frayed silvery tips of the awns dangle down and jostle with nearby perennials in June. At three feet high, I let *Salvia sclarea* (clary sage) proliferate here to add its purple color and steeplelike presence. For a different sequence, just below the grass, place mounds of any pincushion dianthus, such as *Dianthus deltoides* (Maiden pink), which is covered with crimson flowers in spring. In late summer, the foliage on the needle-and-thread grass is shiny bleached white and produces loose clumps of lightweight twisted leaves that remind me of tumbleweed. These fine-textured bunches collect at the base of the needle-and-thread grass.

Nassella tenuissima (Mexican feather grass or pony tail grass)—previously classified as *Stipa tenuissima*—grows to about eighteen inches. This grass is native to open grounds in dry locations and also rocky slopes. Because of its wispy nature, the plant's plumes are easily tossed about when any movement comes along. In July, when this grass is very vibrant and glossy, quirky knotted clumps of strawlike foliage are scattered near the tips, which are fun to pull off by the handful. I have found that Mexican feather grass adapts to hot and dry situations, but is also successful in a perennial border, where it likely receives more moisture, making for glossier, greener leaves. However, in a moister locale, this grass may seed itself around. It likes well-drained soils, full sun to light shade.

In early spring, as Mexican feather grass and other plants "wake up," dwarf bulbs, such as *Iris reticulata* or the blue and white flowers of *Scilla siberica* (Siberian squill), planted in irregular rows, peek out from the chilly soils and can be seen through the transparent leaves of the grass. To highlight this area even further in springtime, grow a few dainty rock garden plants; tucked in among the bulbs are *Draba repens* and *D. rigida*. Both stay astonishing low, not more than four inches, and explode with a shower of yellow flowers to enhance the scene.

Alopecurus pratensis 'Variegatus' (variegated foxtail grass) is a low-growing grass that reaches about a foot in height. Its yellow foliage intensifies in full sun. Variegated foxtail grass has not given me any problems for more than a decade. Although it is happy in a meadow environment or a woodland setting with a bit more moisture, it is content in average soil with average moisture. Once in a while, I need to pick out a few weeds that settle in among the foliage. But such minimal tending is all this grass requires. In mid-spring, it produces one-inch-long puffy beige flowers on top of wire-thin stems. For an

---

With a shimmering sky in the background, the narrow leaves of yellow foxtail grass (Alopecurus pratensis *'Aureovariegatus') act as a foil for the stunning blooms of* Iris *'Beverly Sills'.*

effective background plant in full sun or light shade, I choose euphorbia (wood spurge). *Euphorbia amygdaloides* 'Purpurea' has attractive reddish leaves, which have remained evergreen for a few seasons in my garden. In late spring and early summer, like many wood spurges, it produces chartreuse flowers.

Oryzopsis hymenoides (Indian rice grass) is an ornamental grass with a very different appearance than that of variegated foxtail grass in terms of leaf color, seedhead, and overall shape of plant. The plant's common name reflects its use as a grain by Native Americans. Indian rice grass grows about ten inches high and eight inches wide. Its appearance provides a change of pace among the many flamboyantly colored plants in a rock garden. Its bleached filigree seedheads come into bloom in summer and have a shimmering effect when the afternoon sun is setting. Heavy clay soils are to be avoided, but if a small amount of compost is worked into the existing soil to improve drainage, Indian rice grass will be successful.

The intriguing flowers and stems of *Ruschia putterillii* are perfect for surrounding the Indian rice grass. In six years, my specimen has grown to twelve inches high and two feet wide. While they appear succulent, the evergreen stems of *Ruschia* are gnarly and firm to the touch. Its light pink, nickel-sized flowers almost smother the stems in summer. In a spot where I have some shade and slightly more moisture, I treasure growing *Lewisia cotyledon* (Siskiyou lewisia), which some rock gardeners consider an aristocrat of the Rocky Mountains. The plant's rosette, which tightly hugs the ground, is evergreen; its thick leaves are olive green, smeared with ruby-red markings. The lewisia produces pink flowers in summer. Scatter many of these rosettes beneath Indian rice grass and a luminous partnership will ensue.

A little-known grass ideally suited for use as ground cover is *Sesleria* (moor grass). Most varieties adapt easily to small or large gardens. *Sesleria* prefer full sun, but dappled shade or even a half-day of shade will still produce happy plants. There are approximately twenty-seven varieties of this plant, mostly native to Europe and mountainous areas.

Sesleria are subtle grasses. Their unpretentious flowers quietly call you over to look at them. I purchased *Sesleria autumnalis* (autumn moor grass), which grows from northeastern Italy to Albania. In early summer, the plant's tufted foliage is shiny green. Once its silvery-white flowers shoot up in late summer—they are about half the width of a number-two pencil—the plant is still less than two feet high. As with many grasses, plant a few together to increase the impact. For Colorado, a real selling point for *Sesleria* is that it is long-lived and drought-tolerant. If these were more widely available at garden centers, they would definitely fly off the shelves and into home gardens!

Backlit by the sun, golden and ivory particles of Indian rice grass
(Oryzopsis hymenoides) *invite closer study. (photo by Loraine Yeatts)*

A range of drought-tolerant plants pair well with autumn moor grass, from cushiony rock garden gems to hardy mahogany sedums to woolly, gray foliage plants—in particular the fragrant silver-toned artemisia. For years I have grown *Artemisia versicolor* 'Seafoam' (curlicue sage). With minimal care and well-drained soil, it gradually forms a low mat, shaped like a dinner plate, stretching out more than two feet wide and reaching up to eight inches.

Blue grama is an eight- to fifteen-inch clump-forming grass that I use as an alternative to flowers in my rock garden; my eyes enjoy the restful patch of green lines and odd, beige tips sprinkled among the radiant colors and zestful textures of the alpine plants. Grama's inflorescences are slightly curved like a crescent moon and appear from June through September. I leave the unusual flowers on the plants as they weather to a straw color, enjoying their one-of-a-kind flower well into spring. Alongside a few of these grasses, I planted *Helianthemum nummularium* (sunrose). These evergreen cushion-type plants have quarter-sized spring-blooming flowers that cover practically every shade of the rainbow, including raspberry, orange, pink, yellow, and even a sparkling white. Double flowers appear like crinkled tissue paper. No matter which sunrose you choose, the view will be sensational near the blue grama grass. Blue grama grass can also be planted densely and then mowed to a height of three or four inches to create a drought-tolerant lawn.

Bouteloua curtipendula (side-oats grama) grows six to fifteen inches. This clump-forming grass performs well in dry conditions and in a wide range of soils, but does require full sun to display its purple-tinted flowers in June. Side-oats grama, with autumn colors of gold, rust, and purple, fits in wonderfully near the surrounding color of tree-fallen leaves in shades of yellow, maroon, and beige.

Briza media (quaking grass) is an ornamental grass that has obscure flower parts on a par with the blue grama grass. From Eurasia and also plentiful in the British Isles, it is still not widely available at local garden centers in this country. Quaking grass is easy to grow, tolerant of various soil conditions, and also drought-resistant. It forms a clump of greenery about six inches high. Green stems, about a foot high, shoot out from the clump. They are soon overshadowed by the quirky dangly flowers, which resemble puffed oats. Dried, these would make a glorious addition to a dried flower arrangement. I never got the chance to make a dried flower arrangement because suddenly I noticed a brown mound of foliage where the plant used to be! I had kept an eye on it throughout the springtime and it appeared to be doing fine. Then temperatures consistently soared past ninety, and, since it was newly planted, I'm guessing that it didn't receive enough moisture initially. Not to be deterred, I will try it again, tending the plant more closely next time.

Koeleria (hair grass) is named after G. L. Koeler (1765–1806), a botanist whose passion was grasses. Of the twenty-five or so annual and perennial varieties of this grass, I grow two perennial forms. *Koeleria macrantha* (June grass) mats down a bit in winter, but once April showers have passed, eight-inch-high tufts of bright green suddenly stand proudly and look stunning above a sheet of red and gray pea gravel. In June, silvery, greenish purple plumes appear. The plumes are not as robust or long-lasting as those of *Miscanthus* or *Panicum* grasses; however, they are still attractive as they pulsate in the summertime breezes. Of all the different grasses I grow, I find the plumes on June grass to be the finest in texture, light and silky as feathers, as I gently drag the plumes between my fingers. Before fall sets in, its seedheads are shattered by wind and heat. June grass does spread, but only a small amount each year. A persistent grass, native to the prairie and rocky soils, it returns without fail each year, asking for only the driest spot in your garden, good drainage, and sun. Heavy clay soils or soils with much compost added should be avoided. June grass would grow in partial shade if the drainage were impeccable.

There are many companion plants for June grass. Diverse choices bring in added height and color. From Siberia, *Allium caeruleum*, a bulb that over time forms dense clumps of golf ball–sized powder-blue flowers on stems that are two feet tall, is great as a backdrop for the June grass. The flowers appear in early summer, then fade to an ivory tint toward the end of the summer. At that time, before the tan plumes of the June grass are scattered by the wind, enjoy the exuberant features of *Kniphofia* 'Alcazar' (torch lily). This long-blooming perennial, with grasslike green foliage, is loaded with orange-red spikes, which seem to shoot up like fireworks on the Fourth of July, reaching up to three feet tall. Sunflowers, too, are another flower to plant near June grass.

The other *Koeleria* I grow is somewhat unusual, not even mentioned in most grass books, but nonetheless a gem. *Koeleria brevis*, as the species name hints, is indeed brief. Its green cohesive tuft reaches a mere few inches off the ground; above it, rising over a foot tall, is its unswerving vertical stem, topped off by a half-inch-long silvery-green, cottonlike floret. When I gently touch its pinnacle, puffs of cloudy dust spring forth.

RIGHT: *Numerous spikelets of side-oats grama* (Bouteloua curtipendula) *protrude mostly on one side of this dryland grass. (photo by David Winger)*

Due to its tiny size, one of these grasses does not create a show. I suggest planting a half dozen or more to add liveliness to a rock garden or other small dry area. Full sun, along with good drainage and dry conditions, is ideal for this grass.

One bright, sunny June day, while visiting a nursery well-known for its unusual stock, I stumbled upon an unfamiliar grass in a test bed and was told it was *Koeleria glauca* (blue hair grass). The top few inches of the plant's erect panicles were walnut tan and meatier than the other two *Koeleria* selections I grow.

When I purchase this grass, I'll plant it in a splendid location. I have a large patch of *Artemisia stellerana* 'Silver Brocade' (silver brocade dusty miller) at the base of one of my red stone walls. Three or four of these barely foot-tall grasses with their tan plumes would accent the area, offering up tempting textures to tantalize any viewer's eyes!

Imperata cylindrica var. *koenigii* 'Red Baron' (Japanese blood grass) is a familiar sight in Japan, where it naturally receives adequate moisture (although once established it can be drought-tolerant). Kurt Bluemel's nursery gave it the moniker 'Red Baron'. In regard to hardiness, this grass has gotten mixed reviews. Some people in the Denver Metro area have had success growing it; others have not. It survived two years in my garden. A protected spot might be necessary, and if temperatures fall to ten or twenty degrees below zero the plant may die. But for gardeners who wish to try Japanese blood grass, it has a lot to offer.

The foliage of Japanese blood grass can emerge red and green, but sometimes is a solid mass of deep red color, which may increase in intensity in summer and into fall. Size-wise, in cold climates it will stay in the fifteen-inch range. It rarely flowers, but if it does, its fall-blooming flowers appear on the top few inches, silky soft–looking in a shade of off-white. The main allure of this grass is its brazen foliage. Plant Japanese blood grass in groupings of a half dozen or more. This grass would be especially attractive toward the front of a group of evergreens. 'Red Baron' spreads slowly by shallow moving rhizomes. Make certain your plant is not *Imperata cylindrica* var. *major,* a variety that spreads fast in warm tropical climates (although the likelihood of finding the fast-spreading form in the colder Rocky Mountain region is fairly remote).

Many low-growing grasses are great as fillers for sunny spots. These tufted plants clutch the earth and then pierce the empty air with their precise lines, plumes, and colors.

Annual Grasses and Grasslike Plants

Generally speaking, I don't do much with annuals—grasses or otherwise. I'm not into planting the same or different plants year after year; I prefer the ease of perennials.

However, I like to break my own rules and buy an annual if I'm attracted to it at the nursery or someone, likely a fellow gardener, raves about a plant that sounds so irresistible I must have it. This happened when a nursery owner told me about *Salvia guaranitica* 'Black and Blue', a two-foot-tall gem with grape-purple tubular flowers and deep green, large lobed leaves. The special appeal of this annual was its drought tolerance. I also purchased *Lagurus ovatus* (rabbit tail grass), an annual grass. It had a come-hither look in its small four-inch pot, with a light green flowering tip that resembled a rabbit's foot. I flashed back to when I was a child and had a key chain with a "lucky" rabbit's foot attached. Rabbit tail grass grows to twelve inches, and once dried, the floral top portion remains intact, making it possible to use this grass in winter bouquets.

Two annual grasses that would sell at garden shops of any kind are *Rhynchelytrum nerviglume* ('Pink Crystals' ruby grass) and *Pennisetum glaucum* 'Purple Majesty' ('Purple Majesty' fountain grass). Ruby grass was a Plant Select® plant in 1998. The Denver Botanic Gardens, Colorado State University, and other landscape and nursery professionals choose these plants cooperatively because, after years of testing in the rugged

*Japanese blood grass (*Imperata cylindrica* var. koenigii 'Red Baron') produces brilliant red color from late summer into fall. (photo by Andrew Pierce)*

and fluctuating climate of the Rocky Mountain region, they have been found to be successful. As noted, grasses are often overlooked at garden centers because they seem unappealing in their boring black pots, and these annuals get treated the same way. If you try ruby grass, you won't regret it. It tops out at two feet adorned with pink plumes that shimmer under a hot sun.

'Purple Majesty' is another sun-loving grass, although strictly speaking it is in the grain family, categorized as ornamental millet. The grass grows to approximately three to four feet and likes little to average moisture. Its flowers resemble cornstalks, with a strong purple-red coloring, while the seedheads look like purple cattails. I like the idea of planting this grass among huge sunflowers—the yellow and purple flowers could immerse themselves in each other, creating a spectacular scene for the back of any border.

Pennisetum setaceum (annual or tender fountain grass) lasts only one season in regions where temperatures dip below fifty degrees. In late May, I still had a few open

---

'Pink Crystals' ruby grass (Rhynchelytrum nerviglume) *is weedy in tropical climates, but in Colorado it behaves beautifully as an annual in front of fall-blooming black-eyed Susans. (photo by Andrew Pierce)*

As the foliage of 'Purple Majesty' fountain grass (Pennisetum glaucum 'Purple Majesty') matures, the color is a mixture of deep purple and green. The sturdy flower fills out to a reddish brown.

spaces of bare soil, which I wanted to fill with something, so I bought annual fountain grass, which I had never used. When I noticed its pink flowers at a nursery, I decided to sample it. In fact, as I examined the plant more closely when I arrived home, I realized that I had bought *Pennisetum setaceum* 'Rubrum' (purple fountain grass). In addition to the plant's pink flowers, the foliage beneath its plumes was dark purple. This grass grew to three feet tall, highlighted by its swaying and shapely flowers, which looked to me like dark-colored snakes spilling out of a pot! I liked the strong foliage color contrast that three of these plants created when seen by surrounding perennial greenery and rose foliage, as well as near *Artemisia cana* (silver sage), which added a sprinkle of silver to the panorama. I may buy more purple fountain grass in the future. Next time, I will plant it near *Iris pallida* 'Variegata', whose paper-thin foliage is exquisitely striped with well-defined lines of green, which change to light green and then creamy yellow. While I admire the compatible foliage of these two diverse plants, I'm sure the children in the neighborhood, all smiles and wide glimmering eyes, will salivate over the grape juice scent of the purple iris flowers when they bloom in June.

Annual grasses provide instant gratification; within weeks of planting they billow with color and texture and quickly cover an area. In addition, because they are often shorter in stature than perennial grasses, they work well in various-sized pots. Centered in a pot among colorful annuals, their simple forms and diverse hues inject height wherever pots are placed on the patio, balcony, or in the garden.

A number of plants, because of their grasslike shape, fit in visually with true grasses. Some have already been written about in other parts of this book, such as the sedges that were mentioned in Chapter Three and earlier in this chapter and *Ophiopogon planiscapus* 'Nigrescens' (black mondo grass) in Chapter Three. I'll address just a handful of them; otherwise the scope of this book would become too broad.

A few more deserve special note. First on my list is *Iris lactea* (Mongolian iris). Its quarter-inch-wide, foot-long green foliage sprouts from one main clump and produces many leaves, which fan out like a wide-mouth vase or a clump-forming grass. The plant's thin purple flowers appear in the latter part of May; once they have finished blooming, the foliage looks attractive well into fall. In late summer, in back of this

---

*Fountain grass (*Pennisetum setaceum*) is adorned with soft flower heads; cannas in the middle of the grasses add a spark of color.*

Texture galore! The dark green, foot-tall leaves of Mongolian iris (Iris lactea) *burst forth between*
'Silver Frost' artemisia in front and 'Powis Castle' artemisia farther back.
Center stage is a sedum relative, Rhodolia kirilowii.

---

greenery, another perennial, *Limonium lactifolium* (sea lavender) is taking shape, shooting up thin stems, which quickly produce loose panicles of ethereal flowers in rose-pink
or bluish hues. The picture looks otherworldly, because, unless you are an experienced
gardener, the flowers of the sea lavender appear to belong to the iris plants.

The three-foot-long, sword-shaped leaves of *Yucca baccata* (banana yucca) bring a
statuesque form to provide symmetry, drama, and a focal point in a garden. Initially I
planted this yucca in a small pot. It didn't bloom for seven years. But I was more than
bewitched by its sharp, thick, pointy leaves, as well as by the hair-thin curls on the leaf
margins. At one point I chatted with Kelly Grummons, horticulturist and co-owner of
Timberline Gardens in Arvada, Colorado. I brought up my quandary surrounding the

yucca; he informed me that a young yucca might take seven to ten years to produce its distinctive banana-shaped white blooms.

In the company of the yucca are a host of plants that thrive in low-water conditions. *Papaver triniifolium* (Armenian poppy) has endeared itself to me for many years, since it was one of the first plants I gathered seed from when I volunteered at the Denver Botanic Gardens. This biennial, which grows on rocky slopes in eastern Turkey and surrounding areas, fits in naturally among my rocks. The Armenian poppy begins its life as a silvery-green rosette, five to twelve inches across and up to eight inches tall. The hairy growth on its rosette reminds me of stubble left on my father's face after he had not shaved for a day or so. In its second year, one- to three-foot stalks appear, along with salmon-peachy flowers, which are about two inches in diameter and bloom through much of June into July. Try *Penstemon watsonii* (Watson's beardtongue) near the yucca: the soft hues of its pale lilac and white tubular flowers are appealing juxtaposed with the Gothic shape of the yucca. Finally, in a barrel-shaped trough near the yucca, the

---

*Erect and strong spoonleaf yucca (*Yucca* filimentosa 'Golden Sword') has creamy-white flowers that grow to eight feet high. A copper-colored sedge (*Carex*) winds through the yucca foliage.*

*The lavender-pink flowers of 'Pink Chintz' thyme (*Thymus praecox *'Pink Chintz')*
*swim among the leafy sprouts of blue-eyed grass (*Sisyrinchium bellum*)*
*and atlas daisy (*Anacyclus pyrethrum *var.* depressus *'Gnome').*

charming, tiny *Talinum brevifolium* adds even more diversity. A slow-growing ground cover, this succulent perennial has a coating of pink flowers in summer, and then toward fall, the foliage changes to rusty red. Another yucca selection for architectural structure is spoonleaf yucca (*Yucca filimentosa* 'Golden Sword'). Its thick, yellow and green foliage is spoon-shaped and forms a handsome clump that remains under three feet tall. Although not as drought-tolerant as banana yucca, 'Golden Sword' produces a creamy-white flower stem that may rise six feet tall in summer.

Sisyrinchium angustifolium (blue-eyed grass) is a member of the Iris family. This grasslike plant has star-shaped baby-blue flowers that sport a speck of yellow in the center. The flowers develop in early summer on the extreme tips of the leaves. Blue-eyed grass grows to six inches tall and prefers a bit of moisture. At the base of a rock garden, close to the blue-eyed grass, I've let unrelated plants, such as *Anacyclus*

Mormon tea (Ephedra nevadensis) *bears pipelike, steely blue stems that highlight the bushy flower heads of rabbitbrush* (Chrysothamnus *sp.*).

pyrethrum var. *depressus* 'Gnome' (atlas daisy) and *Thymus praecox* 'Pink Chintz' ('Pink Chintz' thyme) spring up randomly. The many colors converge together, creating an eye-popping scene.

Ephedra nevadensis (Mormon tea) is a thicket of dense foliage that produces a myriad of two-foot-long, skewerlike blue-green stems. The look of this shrub is similar to bamboo. After ten years in my garden, this shrub is four feet high and wide and adds height to a rock garden filled with shorter plants. Accenting the lines of the shrub is a one-ton hunk of smooth stone mottled with gray and red markings.

Cuddling at the base of the Mormon tea, I had a volunteer seedling of *Chrysothamnus* sp. (rabbitbrush) emerge. This accident created a visual spectacle. In fall, the yellow ball-shaped flower heads of the rabbit brush amplify the straight lines of Mormon tea. While each of these plants is lovely by itself, when combined their diversity invites closer inspection.

The yellow, wafer-thin leaves of iris (Iris spuria) *illuminate the needles of dwarf Colorado blue spruce* (Picea pungens 'Globosa') *and the maroon-colored leaves of Korean spice viburnum* (Viburnum carlesii).

A final grasslike plant I'm fond of is *Iris spuria*. This iris, with yellow and blue flowers in summer, blooms after the more traditional bearded iris has flowered. In fall, its spiky green leaves turn yellow and help form a delightful trio when brought together with *Picea pungens* 'Globosa' (dwarf Colorado blue spruce) and the reddish leaves of *Viburnum carlesii* (Korean spice viburnum).

Grasses and grasslike plants bring a wonder of line and movement to any composition of flowers and shrubs. Their crisp and sharp features and varied seedheads engage our eyes, create a sense of complexity in gardens of any style, and fill us with awe.

CHAPTER FIVE

Simple Maintenance for Grasses

Overall, ornamental grasses do not require much attention. Their cultural and climatic requirements are minimal, and they adapt to a wide range of conditions. A few grass tips and guidelines are helpful for the novice gardener, or for anyone curious about soils, techniques for dividing and transplanting, and tools that work best for grass care.

Soil Needs

I never do anything special to care for my grasses. All of them are planted in my flower beds, which means they mingle with perennials,

---

In winter, the tawny foliage of blue oat grass (Helictotrichon sempervirens) waits to be cut down.

shrubs, and in and around rock garden mounds. Over the years, I have added compost, well-rotted manure, and whatever other organic matter has caught my eye. I learned from my mentors that, unless what you mistakenly add is really awful—meaning it is very sandy, or thick muggy clay—practically anything will do. Whatever soil works for your shrubs and perennials will be satisfactory for your grasses, too. In fact, grasses in general can tolerate poorer soil than most perennials. Although grasses may appreciate some compost and good drainage, they have an excellent success rate, even under imperfect conditions.

Planting and Spacing

The simple and carefree approach I discuss above for grasses and soil amending is much like the attitude I have about planting. There are enough *real* stresses in our world; gardening should not be one of them!

Most of the grasses I purchase come in one-gallon black pots. Usually grasses easily slip out of the pots. If they appear tightly root-bound, I slice into the roots with a sharp knife, not much deeper than one inch or so in a few spots. Then I just dig a hole and plant at the same depth the grass was initially, as with any perennial. With grasses, as with all my plants, I make sure to press down securely around the plant's edges so that it bonds with the soil. Pressing down also helps keep the grass from heaving out during fluctuating weather patterns in the extremes of summer and winter.

Spacing of grasses is a personal preference. Some points to consider include the look you desire, the spread at which you want the grasses to fill a space, and your budget. A good rule of thumb for the majority of grasses is to plant them as far apart as their eventual height. Sometimes you'll want to plant just one grass in a spot; other times your eyes, or the site, calls for a massed effect.

The long-term goal with most large ornamental grasses is to appreciate the feathery plumes that the majority of them offer as they mature. To enjoy these plumes, remember to give them room. Most new gardeners err on the side of planting grasses too close to each other. This happens because people find it hard to imagine that anything in such a small pot will really get *that* large! Also remember not to plant the larger varieties too close to walkways and driveways.

Dividing Ornamental Grasses

All grasses, like other plants, grow at different rates from each other. Those grasses with more robust growth need more frequent division than others that grow more slowly. It

LEFT: *Once divided, a section of* Miscanthus sinensis *'Yaku jima' is ready to be replanted.*
RIGHT: *One year the foliage of* Miscanthus sinensis *'Yaku jima' produced reddish leaves that matched the foliage of bloody cranesbill (*Geranium sanguineum*).*

is important to watch their performance as their size increases, especially after the first few years when they begin to expand in width.

Grasses show you when they need to be divided. One signal a grass may exhibit is to begin dying out in the center. Once the grass is cut down, some of the stems will be hollow, break off easily, and reveal dark brown dead growth. Another signal is during the growing season, when the grass blooms: it may not be as floriferous as in the past. You will also want to divide if a grass has grown too big for its spot, squeezing out other special plants. If an area was once in full sun and nearby trees have matured, the now-shaded grass may produce a sparse amount of plumes (or none at all). If a grass is performing very poorly, it may need to be ripped out entirely. Over a number of years, weeds may have crept into the grass. If it is too tedious and time-consuming to pull them out one by one, the best solution may be to remove the grass and buy a new one. Another trip to the nursery—not a big problem for a plant lover!

LEFT: *In early spring, after a month in the ground, a freshly divided clump of blue oat grass* (Helictotrichon sempervirens) *springs forth with new leaves.*
RIGHT: *In June, a detailed picture reveals new striped stems of variegated Japanese silver grass* (Miscanthus sinensis *'Variegatus'*).

In the majority of cases, late winter or early spring is the best time to cut down grass foliage. Be sure to do this simple task even if you are not dividing and moving the grass. Cutting grasses back lets them soar again in spring as they expand with new energy and enthusiasm. Use pruners or loppers, depending on the bulkiness of the grass. A critical point when cutting down grasses is to make sure your tools are sharp. This will help you work more efficiently. For some of the giant grass plants, you may even need a chain saw! I cut grasses down to anywhere from six to twelve inches. Remember that this does not injure them; instead it stimulates them to begin their new growth cycle.

Once the grass is cut down, if you are moving it, the next step is to dig the whole clump out of the ground carefully. Try to keep the clump intact. If the grass is large, work slowly around the edges, getting a bit deeper as you go around it to loosen the plant's grip on the earth. Lift the grass out gently, and push or carry it to an open area that will be accessible to you for dividing the grasses. Sometimes you may need another person's help when digging up and dividing grasses, especially if the plants have been in the same spot for many years. When I divide my grasses, I use a special sharp edging tool, which works wonders! I wear strong-soled shoes, place the sharp edge in the plant, and jump on it a few times. I have also used a shovel, straight-edged or curved, to divide grasses.

Dwayne, a helper in my garden, once recommended a metal tool known as a "mutt." Just a few inches wide, but strong and heavy, the square-shaped mutt is shoved into the grass repeatedly, widening the opening. Choose the tool that works best for you.

Once in a while, because grass clumps may be large and/or awkwardly shaped, you will accidentally rip apart roots or stems. Don't worry! Grasses are resilient and generally remain unscathed by harsh treatment. Keep the best-looking bunches of grass, and toss those that are flimsy. Depending on the maturity of the grass, divide the plant into as many clumps as you desire to replant elsewhere in the garden or to give to gardening friends. Plant at the same depth as the initial clump, and give divided clumps a good drink of water to get them established again.

By dividing your mature grass plants, you will eliminate (or at least decrease) the additional cost and hassle of buying more, and it is a recycling process that benefits both the environment and your senses! Maintaining perennial ornamental grasses takes only these few simple steps. By following them, you can have grasses waving in your garden for years.

In mid-May, alongside meadow sage (Salvia nemerosa), *Miscanthus sinensis* 'Yaku jima' *surges upward as new growth emerges among last year's old stems.*

Quick-Reference Grass Chart

BOTANICAL NAME	COMMON NAME	HEIGHT	WATER NEEDS	COLOR	ADDITIONAL COMMENTS	EXPOSURE	ANNUAL OR PERENNIAL	ZONE
Alopecurus pratensis 'Variegatus'	Variegated foxtail grass	1'	Dry to medium	Unique, thin and smooth, 2-inch-long flower heads	Long-lived attractive ground cover	Full sun to part shade	Perennial	4
Andropogon gerardii	Big bluestem	4–8'	Adaptable/dry or moist soils	Blue-green in summer—fall color is copper-red	Upright and strictly clump forming	Full sun	Perennial	3
Arrhenatherum elatius subsp. *bulbosum* 'Variegatum'	Bulbous oat grass	1'	Dry to medium	Insignificant	Elegant, easily managed	Part shade	Perennial	4
Arundo donax	Giant reed	10–14'	Medium	Infrequent pink cast, drying to silver	Needs space, mulch in cold climates	Full sun	Perennial	6
Bouteloua curtipendula	Side-oats grama	2–3'	Dry to medium	Golden, protruding spikelets, mostly on one side	Great in mass	Full sun	Perennial	4
Bouteloua gracilis	Blue grama, mosquito grass	15"	Dry	Oatlike spikelets	Great in mass	Full sun	Perennial	3
Briza media	Quaking grass, rattle grass	12"	Adaptable to various soils	Oatlike spikelets	Semi-evergreen in cold climates, tricky to grow	Full sun to part shade	Perennial	4
Bromus benekenii	Brome grass	15"	Dry to medium	Wispy seedheads	Aggressive spreader, difficult to find	Full sun to part shade	Perennial	4
Buchloe dactyloides	Buffalo grass	4–8"	Dry to medium	Fine texture	Excellent replacement for bluegrass	Full sun to part shade	Perennial	4
Calamagrostis acutiflora 'Karl Foerster'	Feather reed grass	3–5'	Dry to medium	Feathery, pink-tinted plumes	Excellent for small, narrow spaces	Full sun	Perennial	4
Calamagrostis acutiflora 'Overdam'	Variegated feather reed grass	3–4'	Dry to medium	Flowers similar to 'Karl Foerster'		Full sun	Perennial	4
Calamagrostis brachytricha	Korean feather reed grass	3–4'	Dry to medium	Puffy, pink-tinted flowers	Slow to mature. Rich green leaves are showy as it matures.	Full sun to part shade	Perennial	4
Carex buchananii	Leather leaf sedge	2', vertical, slight bend at top	Medium	No flower—known for coppery-colored foliage	Contrast with colorful flowers or silver foliage otherwise plants look dead. Good drainage needed.	Full sun	Perennial	5
Carex comans	New Zealand hair sedge	1–2', very flowing	Medium	Slight flower—known more for coppery foliage	Divide often to increase coloration	Full sun	Perennial	5
Carex conica 'Snowline'	None	6"	Medium	Dense tuft, no significant flower	Slow growing, great accent near red flagstone, good variegation	Part shade	Perennial	5
Carex morrowii 'Variegata'	Variegated Japanese sedge	8"	Medium	Strong variegation—no significant flower	Mass several together—easy and adaptable. Good choice for shady ground cover.	Part shade	Perennial	5

Botanical name	Common name	Height	Moisture	Flower	Comments	Light	Type	Zone
Carex muskingumensis	Palm sedge	18"–3'	Medium	½-inch-long tan, uncommon flower	Taller in sun. Invasive if too much moisture. Rich green summer foliage.	Full sun to part shade	Perennial	4
Carex muskingumensis 'Oehme'	Variegated palm sedge	2'	Medium	None	Unique lime-green foliage	Full sun to part shade	Perennial	4
Carex pendula	Weeping sedge, great drooping sedge	3–4'	Medium	5-inch-long and tan drooping florets	Dramatic in bloom, invasive with too much moisture.	Part shade	Perennial	4
Carex tumulicola	Berkeley sedge	15"	Dry to medium	Small, distinctive greenish flowers on tips of leaves	Deep green foliage, open habit, sometimes evergreen in protected spot, succeeds in dry shade	Part shade	Perennial	5
Chasmanthium latifolium	Northern sea oats	2'	Dry to medium	Bronzy seedheads	Slow to mature, striking florets, succeeds in dry shade	Part shade	Perennial	5
Cortaderia selloana 'Andes Silver'	Pampas grass	4–6'	Medium	Thin whitish plumes	Hardiness in question in cold climates unless well mulched	Full sun	Perennial	6
Cortaderia selloana 'Patagonia'	Pampas grass	4–6'	Medium	Fluffy whitish plumes	Hardiness in question in cold climates unless well mulched	Full sun	Perennial	6
Deschampsia cespitosa	Tufted hair grass	3'	Dry to medium	Thin, threadlike texture	Lovely when grouped or excellent as a specimen	Full sun to part shade	Perennial	4
Deschampsia cespitosa 'Bronze Veil'	'Bronze Veil' tufted hair grass	2–3'	Medium	Bronzy cast	Robust flowers	Full sun to part shade	Perennial	4
Deschampsia cespitosa 'Fairy's Joke'	'Fairy's Joke' tufted hair grass	2'	Dry to medium	Tiny plantlets are the inflorescences	Distinctive florets—do not enrich with too much compost, otherwise grass will be invasive	Full sun	Perennial	4
Deschampsia flexuosa	Crinkled hair grass	18"–2'	Dry to medium	Thin, hairlike texture	Adaptable to various soils	Full sun to dry shade	Perennial	4
Eragrostis spectabilis	Purple love grass	2'	Dry to medium, drought-tolerant	Fine-textured panicles touched purple	Adaptable in most soils—even if poorly drained. Cut off flowers when finished blooming to halt spreading.	Full sun	Perennial	5
Eragrostis trichoides	Sand love grass	2–4'	Dry to medium, drought-tolerant	Flowers tinged pink	Likes well-drained soil, spreads manageably	Full sun	Perennial	5
Festuca glauca Strong blues— 'Elijah Blue' 'Boulder Blue' 'Sea Urchin'	Blue fescue	5–12"	Dry to medium	Tufts of foliage are various shades of blue in spring, flowers are mostly tan in fall	Prefers well-drained soil. Divide every 2 or 3 years to encourage fresh vibrant growth.	Full sun	Perennial	4
Hakonechloa macra 'Aureola'	Hakone grass	1'	Medium to moist	Known for foliage variegation	Fussy in cold climates	Part shade	Perennial	6
Helictotrichon sempervirens	Blue oat grass	2–4½' with plumes	Dry to medium	Beige blooms	Don't divide too frequently—every 5 to 7 years.	Full sun	Perennial	4
Holcus lanatus	Velvet grass	3'	Medium	Airy, whitish plumes	Aggressive	Full sun	Perennial	5
Holcus mollis 'Variegatus'	Variegated creeping soft grass	6"	Medium	Insignificant	Stunning ground cover	Part shade	Perennial	5

BOTANICAL NAME	COMMON NAME	HEIGHT	WATER NEEDS	COLOR	ADDITIONAL COMMENTS	EXPOSURE	ANNUAL OR PERENNIAL	ZONE
Imperata cylindrical var. koenigii 'Red Baron'	Japanese blood grass	1'	Medium	Insignificant	Fussy, needs protection	Full sun to part shade	Perennial	5
Koeleria macrantha	June grass	2–3'	Dry to medium	4-inch-long plumes	Needs another flower to contrast the plumes. Slow to establish.	Full sun	Perennial	4
Lagurus ovatus	Rabbit tail grass	1'	Dry to medium	Fluffy greenish flowers	Small clump former, nice in dry arrangements	Full sun	Annual	9
Luzula sylvatica	Greater woodrush	1'	Medium	Small bell-like tan flowers	Good clump former, thickish leaves, uncommon companion for ferns and hostas	Part shade	Perennial	4
Miscanthus sinensis 'Adagio'	None	4'	Medium	Tinted red blooms	Similar to 'Yaku jima' but the blooms reach out beyond the foliage like 'Graziella', good yellow fall color	Full sun	Perennial	5
Miscanthus sinensis 'Graziella'	None	4'	Medium	Silvery white	Reddish fall color, narrow form	Full sun	Perennial	5
Miscanthus sinensis 'Morning Light'	None	4–5'	Medium	Faint pink blooms	Fine-textured leaves	Full sun to light shade	Perennial	5
Miscanthus sinensis 'Strictus'	Porcupine grass	5'	Medium	Reddish blooms	Sturdy, distinctive foliage	Full sun	Perennial	5
Miscanthus sinensis 'Variegatus'	Variegated Japanese silver grass	5'	Medium	Reddish blooms	Flowering not consistent in cold climates, although superb foliage makes up for lack of blooms	Full sun	Perennial	5
Miscanthus sinensis 'Yaku jima'	None	4'	Medium	Refined delicate and symmetrical plumes	Mingles well with shrub roses, long-lived if divided every 4 to 5 years. Sometimes red tones in fall.	Full sun	Perennial	5
Molinia caerulea subsp. *arundinacea* 'Skyracer'	Tall purple moor grass	4'	Dry to medium	Unusual textured flowers	Rich orange-red fall color	Full sun	Perennial	4
Muhlenbergia sp.	None	4'	Medium	Delicate open blooms	Most species not reliably cold-hardy	Full sun to light shade	Perennial	6
Nassella tenuissima	Pony tail grass, Mexican feather grass	2'	Dry to medium, very adaptable	Silky, whitish plumes	Too much moisture causes aggressive behavior. Some reseeding even in dry locations.	Full sun to light shade	Perennial	5
Oryzopsis hymenoides	Indian rice grass	1'	Dry	Fraile but refined, off-white floral display	Excellent for rock garden	Full sun	Perennial	4
Panicum virgatum 'Cloud Nine'	Tall switch grass	5–6'	Dryish to medium	Abundant plumes	Mass several together for strong visual display	Full sun	Perennial	4

Botanical name	Common name	Height	Moisture	Flowers	Comments	Light	Type	Zone
Panicum virgatum 'Haense Herms'	Red switch grass	3'	Dryish to medium	Tiny, delicate plumes	Distinctive red and green foliage in autumn	Full sun	Perennial	4
Panicum virgatum 'Heavy Metal'	Blue switch grass	3–4'	Dryish to medium	Light pink plumes	Strong vertical presence. Divide every 5 to 7 years.	Full sun	Perennial	4
Panicum virgatum 'Prairie Sky'	Blue switch grass	3–4'	Dryish to medium	Fine-textured seedheads	Blue-green foliage—slightly thick—about ½ inch	Full sun	Perennial	4
Panicum virgatum 'Shenandoah'	Red switch grass	2–3'	Dryish to medium	Off-white thin plumes	Excellent burgundy fall color	Full sun	Perennial	4
Pennisetum alopecuroides	Fountain grass	3–4'	Medium	Off-white flowers	Superior choice for backlighting. Mix with fall flowers.	Full sun	Perennial	5
Pennisetum alopecuroides 'Moudry'	'Moudry' fountain grass	2–3'	Medium	Dark purple, almost blackish plumes	Attractive yellowish fall color, even without plumes	Full sun	Perennial	9
Pennisetum glaucum 'Purple Majesty'	'Purple Majesty' fountain grass	4–5'	Medium	Robust flowers	Reddish purple foliage, thick leaves	Full sun	Annual	9
Pennisetum setaceum	Tender or annual fountain grass	3–4'	Medium	Whitish to pale pink flowers	Visually effective when massed especially near low-growing annuals	Full sun	Annual	9
Pennisetum setaceum 'Rubrum'	Purple fountain grass	3–4'	Medium	5-inch-long purplish flowers	Deep purple foliage, excellent in large groups	Full sun	Annual	9
Phalaris arundinacea picta	Ribbon grass	1'	Dry to medium	Insignificant	Aggressive—contain with wall or other strong barrier	Full sun to part shade	Perennial	4
Rhynchelytrum nerviglume	'Pink Crystals' ruby grass	1'	Medium	Feathery pink silvery plumes	Mass with taller perennials	Full sun to part shade	Annual	9
Saccharum ravennae	Hardy pampas grass	7–12'	Medium	Foot-long, stout blooms	Excellent accent or screen	Full sun	Perennial	5
Schizachyrium scoparium	Little bluestem	2–3'	Dry to medium	Delicate, narrow plumes, most effective in groups	Foliage variable—various shades of green and blue—strong reddish leaves in fall. Prefers good drainage.	Full sun	Perennial	4
Sesleria autumnalis	Autumn moor grass	20"	Medium	Slender tan plumes	Easy care, weeping green foliage	Full sun to part shade	Perennial	4
Spartina pectinata	Prairie cord grass	2–3'	Medium to moist	Golden plumes	Golden foliage, dramatic accent near a pond	Full sun to part shade	Perennial	4
Spodiopogon sibericus	Siberian graybeard	3–4'	Medium	Cone-shaped, fine-textured blooms	Once established, easy to grow. Unusual, difficult to find.	Full sun to part shade	Perennial	4
Sporobolus heterolepis	Prairie dropseed	15"	Dry to medium	Silvery robust plumes	Slender green foliage, strong red fall color, adaptable to most soils	Full sun to part shade	Perennial	4

Mail-Order Sources for Native and Ornamental Grasses

Forestfarm
990 Tetherow Road
Williams, OR 97544-9599
Phone: (541) 846-7269
Website: www.forestfarm.com

Granite Seed
1697 W. 2100 North
Lehi, UT 84043
Phone: (801) 768-4422
Website: www.graniteseed.com

Kurt Bluemel, Inc.
2740 Green Lane
Baldwin, MD 21013-9523
Phone: (800) 498-1560

Prairie Nursery
P.O. Box 306
Westfield, WI 53964
Phone: (800) 476-9453
Website: www.prairienursery.com

Prairie Moon Nursery
31837 Bur Oak Lane
Winona, MN 55987-9515
Phone: (866) 417-8156
Website: www.prairiemoon.com

High Country Gardens
2902 Rufina Street
Sante Fe, NM 87507-2929
Phone: (800) 925-9387
Website: www.highcountrygardens.com

Related Reading

Armitage, Allan M. *Armitage's Garden Perennials.* Portland, OR: Timber Press, 2000.

Bailey, Liberty Hyde, and Ethel Zoe Bailey. Revised and expanded by the staff of Liberty Hyde Bailey Hortorium. *Hortus Third: A Concise Dictionary of Plants Cultivated in the United States and Canada.* New York: Macmillan, 1976.

Brawner, Mikl. "The Drought Response?" *Colorado Gardener* (Feb./March 2003), pp.12–14.

Christopher, Thomas. *Water-Wise Gardens: America's Backyard Revolution.* New York: Simon and Schuster, 1994.

The Colorado Native Plant Society. *Rare Plants of Colorado.* Helena, MT: Falcon Press Publishing Co., Inc., in cooperation with the Rocky Mountain Nature Association, 1997.

Darke, Rick. *The Color Encyclopedia of Ornamental Grasses.* London: The Orion Publishing Group, 1999.

Darke, Rick (consulting ed.), and Mark Griffiths (series ed.). *Manual of Grasses.* Portland, OR: Timber Press, 1994.

Denver Water. *Xeriscape Plant Guide.* Golden, CO: Fulcrum Publishing, 1996.

Elliott, Clarence. *Rock Garden Plants.* London: E. Arnold & Co., 1996.

Greenlee, John. *The Encyclopedia of Ornamental Grasses.* Emmaus, PA: Rodale Press, 1992.

Knopf, Jim. *The Xeriscape Flower Gardener.* Boulder, CO: Johnson Books, 1991.

Lacy, Allen. "Ornamental Grasses." *Horticulture* (Nov. 1990), Vol.68, no.11.

Loewer, Peter. *The Annual Garden.* Emmaus, PA: Rodale Press, 1995.

Madson, John. *Where the Sky Began.* Ames: Iowa State University Press, 1996.

Ottesen, Carole. *Ornamental Grasses: The Amber Wave.* San Francisco: McGraw-Hill Publishing Co., 1989.

Pesman, M. Walter. *Meet the Natives.* Denver, CO: Roberts Rinehart Publishers, 1992.

Thomas, Graham Stuart. *The Rock Garden and Its Plants: From Grotto to Alpine House.* Portland, OR: Timber Press, 1989.

Williams, Jean, ed. *Rocky Mountain Alpines.* Portland, OR: Timber Press, 1996.

Index

Note: Page numbers in **bold** indicate illustrations.

planet ea

AMAZING ANIMALS OF THE RAINFOREST

By Tracey West

SCHOLASTIC INC.

New York   Toronto   London   Auckland   Sydney
Mexico City   New Delhi   Hong Kong   Buenos Aires

Contents

What Is a Rainforest?

A rainforest is a tropical forest, usually of tall, densely growing evergreen trees in an area of high annual rainfall. It is home to millions of plants and animals. In a rainforest, you'll find these four things:

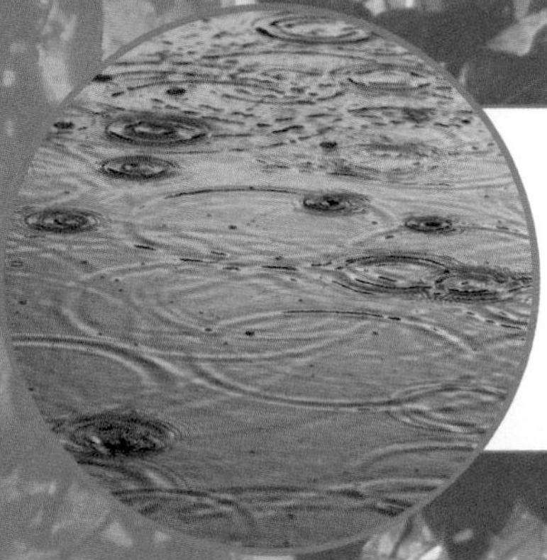

Rain:

It rains between 65 and 100 inches a year in a rainforest, more than anywhere else in the world.

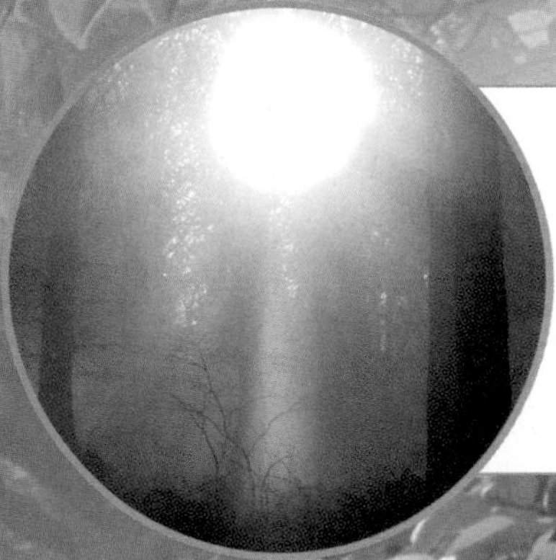

Sun:

Many rainforests are located in tropical areas near the equator. Here the sun shines for 12 hours a day, which helps plants grow.

Plants:

Rainforests only cover 3 percent of the Earth's surface, but are home to one-half of the world's plants. A typical rainforest is filled with trees, vines, and flowers that grow so closely together that if you're on the rainforest floor, the canopy of the trees hides the sky above.

Animals:

Scientists estimate that more than half of all the world's animals live in rainforests. There are countless species of fish that live in the rivers that act as arteries of any rainforest.

Types of Rainforests

There are five basic types of tropical rainforests in the world.

Lowland Tropical Forest:

These are the largest areas of rainforest in the world. Clustered close to the equator, they contain millions of plants that grow very close together. In these forests, the trees stay green all year round.

Tropical Deciduous Forest:

These forests are located in tropical areas of the world, such as Jalisco, Mexico, but they're a little farther away from the equator than the lowland forests. There is usually a dry period for a few months, causing some of the trees to shed their leaves.

Flooded Forest:

In some parts of the world, rivers near rainforests flood once a year. This happens in the Amazon basin, when the Amazon river floods its banks. For about half the year, the rainforest floor is submerged, and the habitat changes. New sources of food are available, and new migration patterns develop as a result.

Tropical Mountain Forest:

Also called a cloud forest, these rainforests grow on high mountaintops throughout the world. The temperature is cooler here than in lowland rainforests, but they are still very wet places. The humidity is often at 100%, and the moisture from the fog and clouds allows epiphytes—like orchids, mosses, and other plants that attach themselves to other plants—to flourish.

Mangrove Forest:

These special forests can be found where the land meets the sea, such as in areas of South Florida, or Southeast Asia. Mangrove trees grow in the water and the roots of the trees grow up out of the mud so they can absorb oxygen. These unique environments provide a safe nursery ground for fish, and support a wide variety of birds, reptiles, and shellfish.

Rainforest Layers

A rainforest can be divided into different layers, each one home to different kinds of animals and plants. The animals in this scrapbook are grouped together according to the layers they live in.

Water:

This is the bottom layer of a Flooded Forest or Mangrove Forest. Many river-dwelling animals, such as freshwater dolphins, migrate to these forests when the rivers flood.

Forest Floor:

This is the bottom layer of a typical rainforest. The trees here grow very tall, so as to compete for as much sunlight as possible. This is why very little sunlight reaches this layer (approximately 2%). The forest floor is home to lots of insects as well as large, land-dwelling animals such as gorillas and elephants.

Understory:

This is the area above the ground but underneath the leaves of the trees. Like the forest floor, the understory is cool and dark. Jaguars and leopards live in branches of the trees here.

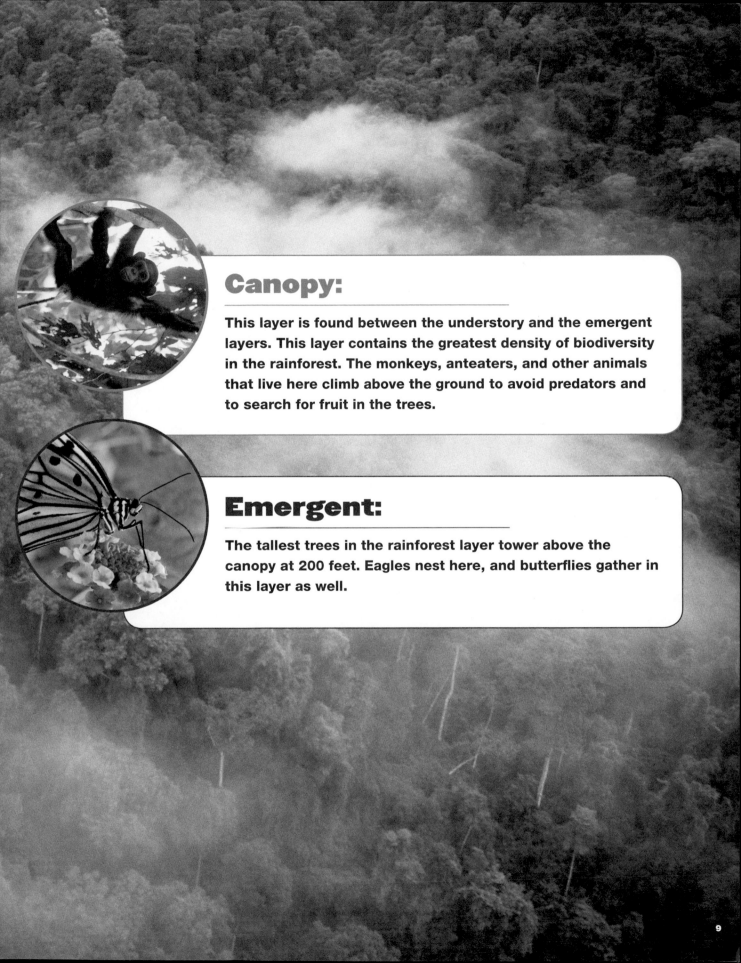

Canopy:

This layer is found between the understory and the emergent layers. This layer contains the greatest density of biodiversity in the rainforest. The monkeys, anteaters, and other animals that live here climb above the ground to avoid predators and to search for fruit in the trees.

Emergent:

The tallest trees in the rainforest layer tower above the canopy at 200 feet. Eagles nest here, and butterflies gather in this layer as well.

ORANGE SPOT FRESHWATER STINGRAY

ANATOMY 101

- Gills on top of the head let the stingray breathe while it is partially buried in sand or mud.
- Having a mouth on your belly might seem weird to you, but it's useful for the stingray. It can move its body over prey, and then suck it up!
- This fish can get as big as 3 feet long from head to tail.
- This tail isn't just sharp—it's venomous! The stingray mostly uses its stinger to defend itself.

FISH

Species: *Potamortrygon motoro*

Also known as: South American freshwater stingray

Average weight: 8 to 10 pounds

Average size: 18 inches in diameter; as long as 3 feet from head to tail

Where it lives: The Amazon River

Watch that *stinger!* **This relative of a shark doesn't have teeth, but its sharp tail is a painful weapon.**

A piranha's teeth are shaped like triangles that fit together like the blades of a scissor.

This rainforest species has the *sharpest* **teeth and most powerful jaws of any piranha.**

RED-BELLIED PIRANHA

School's In

These piranhas travel together in large schools, mainly eating small fish and fruit, but if they come across a large animal that's sick or vulnerable, they can quickly tear it apart with their long teeth.

FISH

Species: *Pygocentrus nattereri*

Maximum weight: Up to 8 pounds

Maximum length: 12 to 24 inches

Where it lives: Rivers in South America

Favorite meal: Other fish, insects

The tucuxi (pronounced: too-koo-shee) looks a lot like a bottlenose dolphin, but it's much smaller—usually about four feet long.

TUCUXI

When a rainforest **floods**, this freshwater *"river dolphin"* migrates into the area to *search for food*.

MAMMAL

Species: *Sotallia fluviatillis*

Also known as: River dolphin

Average weight: About 100 pounds

Average length: 4 to 5 feet

Where it lives: Rivers, bays, and lakes in South America

Favorite meal: Fish

People *fish* for this animal in the **rivers** of *South America*.

DORADO

In Argentina, this fish is known as the "tiger of the Paraná," a river that runs through the country. This fish is called this because it fights back when it is caught on a hook by fishermen.

FISH

Species: *Salminus maxillosus*

Average weight: More than 40 pounds

Average length: 39 inches

Where it lives: Rivers in northern Argentina, Brazil, and Bolivia

ANATOMY 101

• Dorado means "golden" in Spanish. This fish gets its name from its striking yellow, orange, and black scales.

• The largest dorado ever caught weighed 75 pounds.

• This carnivorous fish has sharp teeth that help it chow down on smaller fish.

SPECTACLED CAIMAN

This member of the *alligator* family spends **most** of its life in **water**.

Family Ties

Female spectacled caimans lay their eggs in nests they build on the ground. When the babies hatch, they form groups, and remain together until they're about a year and a half old.

REPTILE

Species: *Caiman crocodilus*

Also known as: Common caiman, tinga

Average length: 3 to 6 feet

Where it lives: Rivers, wetlands, and rainforests in Central and South America

ANATOMY 101

- A bony ridge around the caiman's eyes make people think of eyeglasses, or "spectacles"— that's how it received its name.
- A long, muscular tail propels the spectacled caiman through the water.
- Its webbed feet help the caiman swim.
- Most caimans measure up to 7 or 8 feet long— but some can grow up to 10 feet.

AGOUTI

These *rodents* play a role in keeping the *rainforest* alive.

MAMMAL
Species: *Dasyprocta punctata*
Average weight: 2 to 9 pounds
Average length: 16 to 25 inches
Where it lives: Central and South America, east of the Andes Mountains

ANATOMY 101
- This nimble rodent can grow up to 2 feet long and weigh up to 9 pounds.
- The agouti can crack open hard Brazil nutshells with its sharp teeth.
- An agouti's tail is only about an inch long.

Nut Crackers

Brazil nut trees tower over rainforests in South America. Brazil nuts grow inside hard pods that look like coconuts. Agoutis not only eat Brazil nuts, but they help the trees to grow, too. How? They bury extra nuts in the ground to eat later, and the nuts they forget to retrieve sometimes grow into Brazil nut trees.

When danger is near, an agouti will grunt, squeal, and bark to warn others.

Indonesia used to be home to three kinds of tigers: the Bali tiger, the Java tiger, and the Sumatran tiger. Now, both the Bali and the Java tigers have become extinct, and Sumatran tigers are critically endangered.

MAMMAL

Species: *Tigris sumatrae*

Average weight: 265 pounds (males), 200 pounds (females)

Average length: 8 feet (males), 7 feet (females)

Where it lives: Only in Sumatra, an island in Indonesia

Favorite meal: Wild pigs, deer, fish, crocodiles, birds

ANATOMY 101

- Webbing between the toes makes these cats fast swimmers.
- White spots on the back of the tiger's ears are called "eye spots" or "predator spots." They may be used to fool predators attempting to sneak up on the tiger from behind—as these spots can be mistaken for eyes.
- Long whiskers act as sensors to help these tigers move through the thick vegetation on the rainforest floor.
- At night, a Sumatran tiger can see six times better than a human.
- Its dark red coat and closely spaced black stripes camouflage the tiger in the forest.

SUMATRAN TIGER

Fewer than 500 of these tigers inhabit the rainforests of the *Indonesian island* of Sumatra.

BENGAL TIGER

These *tigers* can be found **roaming** the *mangrove forests* of India and **Bangladesh**.

Night Hunters

Bengal tigers hunt at night. Their favorite meals are deer, wild boar, and monkeys. To hunt their prey, they use a stalk and ambush approach. The tigers silently follow their prey and when they are close, they run in to make the kill.

Bengal tigers can eat up to 65 pounds of meat a night.

MAMMAL

Species: *Panthera tigris*

Average weight: 500 pounds (male), 300 pounds (female)

Average length: 10 feet (male), 9 feet (female)

Where it lives: The mangrove forests of India and Bangladesh

Favorite meal: Wild ox and buffalo

These ants turn *leaves* into a special *fungus* they can *eat*.

Fungus Farmers

Leaf-cutter ants live in underground colonies of 3 to 8 million ants! Each ant has a special job.

Foragers: These ants march for miles in search of leaves. They use their sharp jaws to cut the leaves and then bring them back to the colony.

Gardeners: Ants can't digest leaves, so the gardener ants use the leaves to make fungus that they can digest. First, they lick the leaves clean; then they grind them up; and finally they deposit dung on them. Then fungus grows on the dung. Yummy!

Defenders: These soldier ants protect the colony from attack by other ants.

INSECT

Species: *Atta cephalotes*

Average length: About 0.5 inch

Where it lives: Tropical rainforests and other forests in parts of Central America, South America, and North America

LEAF-CUTTER ANTS

GOLIATH BIRD-EATING TARANTULA

When the rainforest floods, the goliath will climb into the trees to stay dry.

Despite its name, this **huge spider** mostly dines on *bugs*, rodents, and **frogs.**

ANATOMY 101

- This spider spans 12 inches wide from leg to leg. That's about the size of a small pizza!
- The tarantula has sharp, tiny hairs on its legs that can be shot at enemies.
- The goliath kills prey with a venomous bite, but don't worry—this poison isn't strong enough to kill humans.

INSECT

Species: *Theraposa blondi*

Average weight of adult male: About 4 ounces

Average length of adult male: About 11 inches

Where it lives: Rainforests on the coast of northeastern South America

MAMMAL

Species: *Loxodonta cyclotis*

Average weight: 3,690 to 7,040 pounds

Average height: About 8 feet

Where it lives: Forests near the equator in Africa

ANATOMY 101

- Their straight tusks are less likely to get caught in the underbrush than the curved tusks of other elephant species.
- When these elephants get hot, they can flap their big ears to fan themselves. Their ears are packed with blood vessels to help them disperse heat quickly and keep them cool.
- They are able to walk quietly through the forest thanks to their wide, padded feet.
- They use their long trunks to do many things: breathe, smell, spray water, uproot trees, pick up food, and—of course!—make noise.

AFRICAN FOREST ELEPHANT

These **elephants** live in forests near the equator in *Central Africa.*

SUMATRAN RHINOCEROS

It might have two *sharp horns*, but this massive mammal is a *peaceful* plant eater.

During the hottest hours of the day, Sumatran rhinos wallow in muddy water to beat the heat.

MAMMAL

Species: *Dicerorhinus sumatrensis*

Also known as: Asian two-horned rhinoceros

Average weight: 0.8 ton

Average length: 8 to 10.5 feet, plus a 20-inch tail

Where it lives: Tropical rainforests in Indonesia

Rhinos in Danger

There are fewer than 400 Sumatran rhinos left in the world today. They've lost habitat from large areas of rainforest that have been cut down.

MAMMAL

Species: *Felis pardalis*

Average weight of adult male: 24 to 35 pounds

Average length of adult male: 28 to 35 inches (not including tail)

Where it lives: from Texas south to Argentina

Solitary Hunters

Ocelots usually live alone. They like to hunt at night for prey such as rabbits, rodents, iguanas, frogs, and small turtles. Even though they are great tree climbers, they prefer to hunt on the ground.

This *nocturnal cat* stays hidden in the rainforest **underbrush** during the *day*.

ANATOMY 101

- The ocelot's coat is considered to be the most beautiful fur of any big cat. This is bad news for the ocelot, which has been hunted for its fur.

OCELOT

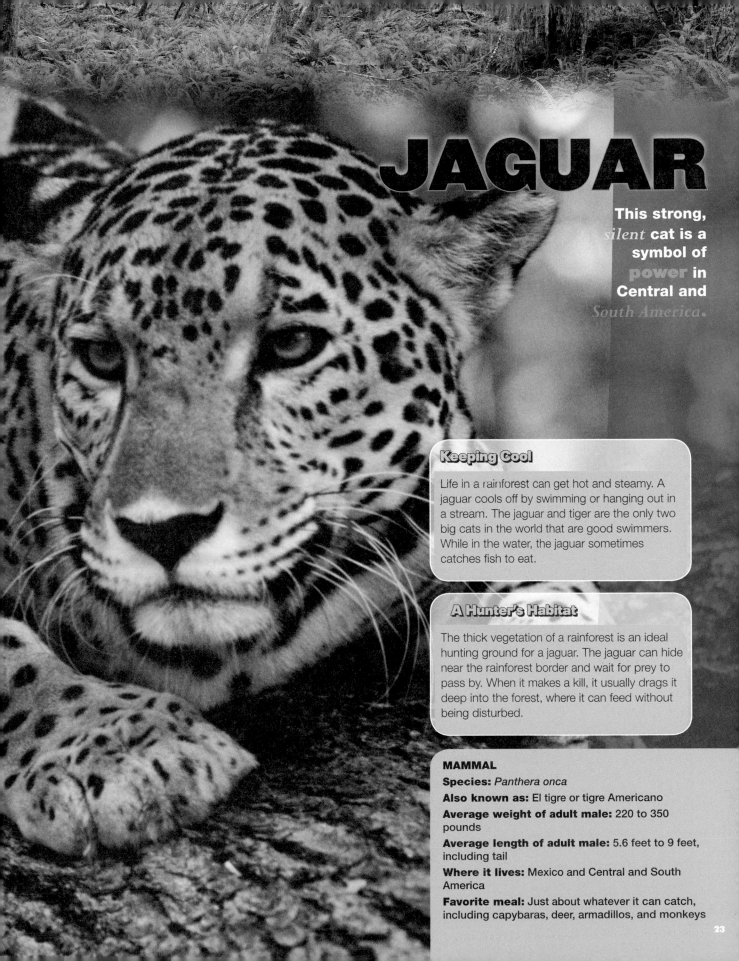

JAGUAR

This strong, *silent* cat is a symbol of power in Central and *South America.*

Keeping Cool

Life in a rainforest can get hot and steamy. A jaguar cools off by swimming or hanging out in a stream. The jaguar and tiger are the only two big cats in the world that are good swimmers. While in the water, the jaguar sometimes catches fish to eat.

A Hunter's Habitat

The thick vegetation of a rainforest is an ideal hunting ground for a jaguar. The jaguar can hide near the rainforest border and wait for prey to pass by. When it makes a kill, it usually drags it deep into the forest, where it can feed without being disturbed.

MAMMAL

Species: *Panthera onca*

Also known as: El tigre or tigre Americano

Average weight of adult male: 220 to 350 pounds

Average length of adult male: 5.6 feet to 9 feet, including tail

Where it lives: Mexico and Central and South America

Favorite meal: Just about whatever it can catch, including capybaras, deer, armadillos, and monkeys

SHORT-TAILED LEAF-NOSED BAT

These **nighttime** flyers help bring destroyed areas of *rainforest* back to **life.**

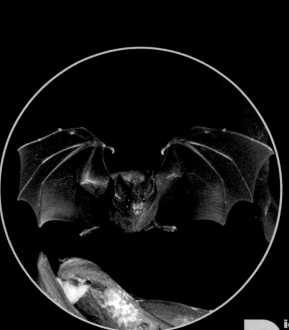

Did You Know?
About one out of every 500 of these bats is bright orange!

MAMMAL

Species: *Carollia perspecillata*

Also known as: Short-tailed fruit bat

Average weight: 0.6 of an ounce

Average length: 1.9 to 2.6 inches

Where it lives: Mexico, Bolivia, Paraguay, Brazil, and the Caribbean Islands

Seed Spreaders

When the sun goes down, short-tailed leaf-nosed bats go to work. The bats fly through the understory looking for fruit to eat. When they find some, they find a safe perch and eat it, seeds and all. When they're done eating, they take a short nap before repeating this cycle again and again — all night long!

As the bat flies through the understory, it carries pollen on its body, pollinating the flowers as it goes. It also poops out the seeds it hasn't digested. These seeds fall to the ground, and new plants grow. A single bat can "plant" as many as 60,000 seeds in one night.

ANATOMY 101
- Jacamars are known for the glittery green feathers on their upper body and upper breast.
- The long, slender bill is sometimes called a "needle beak."

BIRD

Species: *Galbula ruficauda*

Average weight: About 1 ounce

Average length: 9 inches with a 2-inch-long bill

Where it lives: Mexico, Ecuador, Bolivia, Argentina, Colombia, Venezuela, the Guianas, Brazil, and Trinidad and Tobago

Butterflies for Breakfast

You may think a butterfly is beautiful to look at, but when a jacamar sees a butterfly, it sees a meal. When a butterfly flies by, the jacamar chases it, catching it with its beak. Then, the jacamar goes back to its perch, and pounds the butterfly against a branch before gobbling it down.

These colorful *birds* perch on low **shrubs** in the **understory** of the rainforest and hunt for *butterflies* and dragonflies.

RUFOUS-TAILED JACAMAR

Grooming is important to chimps. They often spend hours picking bugs and twigs out of each other's fur.

These apes eat, **sleep**, and *play* in the **trees** of the *rainforest* canopy.

CHIMPANZEE

Chimps have many ways to communicate with each other. They grunt, bark, and make gestures with their hands. They also make a loud noise called a pant-hoot. Each chimp has its own pant-hoot so that the other chimps know which one of them is calling out. A pant-hoot might be used to let other chimps know danger is near, or if food has been found.

They're a Lot Like Us!

Chimpanzees are the closest living relatives to humans. We share more than 98% of the same DNA. Here are some other ways chimps and humans are alike:

• We both live in communities: Chimps live in social groups that contain several dozen members.

• We both use tools: When they need to gather food or water, chimps use sticks, stones, and leaves to help them. They also use sticks as weapons, throwing them at their enemies.

• We're both omnivores: Chimps mostly eat fruits, nuts, and plants, but they also eat insects and eggs, and they sometimes hunt for medium-sized animals.

MAMMAL

Species: *Pan troglodyte*

Average weight: 90 to 120 pounds (male), 60 to 110 pounds (female)

Average height: 4 feet

Where it lives: Tropical rainforests, bamboo forests, swamps, and other areas of Africa

These *long-nosed* monkeys like to **live** near *water*, away from human **settlements**.

Proboscis monkeys have webbing between their fingers that helps them swim. These monkeys can swim underwater, and they're high divers, too! They can leap into the water from the upper branches of trees.

Old vs. New

Monkeys can be divided into two groups: Old World and New World. Old World monkeys, such as the proboscis, have thick tails that help them balance. New World monkeys, such as the capuchin, have tails that they can use to grab things (called prehensile tails).

ANATOMY 101
- The word *proboscis* means "prominent nose."
- This belly may look fat, but it actually holds a large stomach with many chambers. The proboscis monkey eats a special diet of starchy fruits, leaves, and seeds. The food sits around in its belly and ferments for a while before the monkey can digest it.

PROBOSCIS MONKEY

MAMMAL

Species: *Nasalis larvatus*

Average weight: 35 to 48 pounds (males), 15 to 26 pounds (females)

Average length: 27 inches (males), 24 inches (females)

Where it lives: In mangrove forests and some rainforests in Borneo, an island in Southeast Asia

BROWN CAPUCHIN MONKEY

Brown capuchins are thought to be more intelligent than any other monkey.

These **clever** creatures live in the **rainforests** of *South America*.

MAMMAL

Species: *Cebus apella*

Average weight: About 3 to 11 pounds

Average length: 38 inches, including tail

Where it lives: Forests east of the Andes Mountains in South America

Gets Eaten By: Snakes, jaguars, and birds of prey

ANATOMY 101
- Their prehensile tails are like an extra hand or foot; they help the monkeys climb trees in the canopy.
- The brown capuchin has a big jaw so it can eat big pieces of fruit.

It's Good to Be the Leader

Brown capuchins live in small groups of 8 to 15 monkeys. Each group is led by a dominant male. This male leader has a big job. He leads the attack if his group is threatened by predators or other monkeys. On the other hand, the job has its perks: If there is not enough food to go around, the leader gets to eat first.

Tag-a-Longs

Squirrel monkeys like to hang out around brown capuchin monkeys. Why? They follow the capuchins to new food sources. This saves them the job of foraging for food themselves.

BROWN HOWLER MONKEY

What's that sound? It **might** be this monkey's *incredible* call.

Hooooooowl!

The howler monkey's amazing howl can be heard from more than a mile away! A bone in the monkey's neck vibrates, amplifying the sound. Scientists think they howl as a way to mark their territory.

ANATOMY 101

- Even though they're called brown howler monkeys, this monkey's fur can have shades of red, yellow, and orange.
- A prehensile tail allows howlers to hang from trees when they feed.

MAMMAL

Species: *Alouatta guariba*

Average weight: 11 to 17.6 pounds (males), 8.8 to 11 pounds (females)

Average length: About 22 inches plus a 23-inch tail (males), about 18.5 inches plus 21.5-inch tail (females)

Where it lives: Coastal rainforests in Brazil

During the hottest part of the day, brown howler monkeys take a siesta!

Treetop Dwellers

Brown howlers spend most of their time in trees where they eat leaves, flowers, and fruits.

MAMMAL

Species: *Macaca fascicularis*

Average weight: About 14 pounds (male), about 9 pounds (female)

Average length: About 1.8 feet (male), about 1.5 feet (female)

Where it lives: The islands of Southeast Asia and some countries in Asia

Favorite foods: Fruit, crabs, insects, mushrooms, frogs, octopus, shrimp

Seafood Lovers

When these monkeys search for food in mangrove forests, they will scoop up crabs, frogs, shrimp, and octopi.

ANATOMY 101

- A special pouch inside their cheek stores food so the macaque can eat it later.

Water Escape

Long-tailed macaques are good swimmers. They like to live in trees that hang over rivers. If a predator attacks, they jump off the tree into the water and swim to safety.

LONG-TAILED MACAQUE

These *water-loving* monkeys like to **chow down** on seafood.

RUBY-THROATED
HUMMINGBIRD

Fast Flappers

A ruby-throated hummingbird can flap its wings 53 times in just one second! The fast beating of the wings is what makes the "humming" sound hummingbirds are known for.

BIRD

Species: *Archilocus colubris*

Average weight: .07 to .21 ounces

Average length: 3 to 4 inches

Where it lives: North America and Central America

Gets eaten by: Other birds such as loggerhead shrikes, hawks, and blue jays; domestic cats

In *warm* months, you can see this **tropical bird** in parts of *North America*.

ANATOMY 101
- This bird gets its name from the red throat found on males.

These hummingbirds like to eat nectar from flowers—especially red ones.

These common *birds* can be seen **perching** on **branches** in the *canopy*.

BIRD

Species: *Tityra semifasciata*

Average weight: About 3.1 ounces

Average length: About 8 inches

Where it lives: In tropical forests from Mexico down to Bolivia and Brazil

ANATOMY 101
- The red coloring around this bird's eyes and base of the beak forms a colorful "mask."

MASKED
TITYRA

HOATZIN

This *rainforest* dweller looks like a **punk-rock** chicken!

ANATOMY 101

• The hoatzin has bacteria in its gut that slowly breaks down the leaves it eats. This bacteria gives off a really bad smell, which is why it's sometimes called "stinkbird."

BIRD

Species: *Opisthocomus hoazin*

Average weight of adult male: 1.8 pounds

Average length of adult male: 24 to 26 inches

Where it lives: In swamps, mangrove forests, lowland flooded forests, and other places in South America

Favorite foods: The leaves and shoots of plants that grow in swamps and marshes

---

With its *brightly colored* beak, this bird stands out in the **rainforests** of Central and *South America.*

BIRD

Species: *Ramphastos sulfuratus*

Also known as: Bill bird

Average weight: About 14 ounces

Average length: About 26 inches, including its long beak

Where it lives: In Central and South America, from southern Mexico to northern Colombia

Favorite foods: Fruit, insects, lizards, snakes

ANATOMY 101

• The large, colorful bill is what this bird is best known for. Scientists aren't exactly sure why this bill is so big. It's useful for picking and eating fruit, and it may be used as a defensive weapon.

Toucans aren't great flyers, so they hop along from tree to tree.

KEEL-BILLED TOUCAN

Hole Sweet Home

Toucans live in holes in tree trunks. Sometimes they inhabit holes that were made and abandoned by woodpeckers. Oftentimes, a number of toucans will try to fit into one hole. To do that, each toucan will fold its tail over its head to make room for the others.

TREE ANTEATER

ANATOMY 101
- A prehensile tail helps the tree anteater climb trees.
- Tree anteaters have coarse hairs all over their body. This keeps the ants from biting them.
- Inside their long snout is a 16-inch-long tongue with little barbs on it. It's the perfect tool for scooping ants out of an anthill.

Like some *birds*, these mammals nest in **tree** trunks.

MAMMAL
Species: *Tamandua tetradactyla (southern);* *Tamandua mexicana (northern)*

Also known as: Tamandua

Average weight: 90 to 120 pounds (male), 60 to 110 pounds (female)

Average length: 1.8 to 2.9 feet, plus a tail that's about 1.5 feet long

Where it lives: Tropical rainforests, savannas, and other areas ranging from Mexico down to South America

ANATOMY 101
- Powerful muscles in their hands and feet allow these animals to hang from tree branches.

These *big-eyed* mammals **seldom** leave the *rainforest* canopy.

MAMMAL
Species: *Nycticebus pygmaeus*

Average weight: 2 pounds

Average length: 6 to 10 inches

Where it lives: Rainforests in southeast Asian countries and islands, including Thailand, Vietnam, and China

Favorite foods: Large mollusks, birds, small mammals, fruit, lizards, eggs, and insects such as caterpillars and beetles

LESSER SLOW LORIS

ANATOMY 101

- The frog's eyelids are green, so when it sleeps during the day its closed eyes blend with the rest of its body and with the plants around it to hide from predators. If a predator comes near, the frog opens its red eyes, startling the predator, giving the frog a few seconds to escape!

- Frogs can cling to the underside of leaves thanks to suction-cup-like footpads on the bottoms of their feet.

RED-EYED TREE FROG

It's not hard to *guess* how this **canopy dweller** got its name!

This snake's jawbones are attached by stretchy ligaments—kind of like rubber bands. This allows the jaw to stretch open wide enough to swallow prey whole!

How It Kills

In water, the anaconda grabs its prey with its jaws and then coils its long body around its prey until it suffocates it. On land, it hangs in trees, drops down on its prey from above, coils around the animal, and squeezes it to death.

GREEN
ANACONDA

This *green giant* will attack and **eat** just about anything it can get its *jaws* around.

ANATOMY 101

- The green anaconda likes to eat animals that live in water. Its eyes and nostrils are on top of its head, which allows it to breathe, watch, and wait for prey while its body is hidden underwater.

- Pythons can grow longer than green anacondas, but anacondas weigh much more—usually around 300 pounds! That's how they've earned the title of largest snake in the world.

- On average, Anacondas can grow to 20 feet long, but some can get as long as 29 feet!

REPTILE

Species: *Eunectes murinus*

Average weight: 330 pounds

Average length: About 20 feet

Where it lives: Tropical rainforests, swamps, marshes, and streams in South America

HARPY EAGLE

Few **people** have seen this *beautiful* bird of *prey* in the **wild.**

Nests in the Sky

Harpy eagles build their nests at the very top of tall Kapok trees, as high as 140 feet above ground. The nests are built from sticks and branches and lined with green plants and animal fur. Each nest is about 5 feet wide.

BIRD

Species: *Harpia harpyja*

Average weight: 8.5 to 12 pounds (male), 14 to 20 pounds (female)

Average wingspan: Up to 7 feet

Average length of body: 35 to 41 inches

Where it lives: Rainforests in Central and South America, from Mexico to northern Argentina

How It Hunts

Even though the harpy eagles' nests are in the emergent layer of the rainforest, they save energy by hunting in the canopy. First, they perch and wait for prey to appear and then they dive after the prey. Smaller prey, such as iguanas, are brought up to the treetops to be eaten. A harpy eagle can only carry about half of its weight, so the heavier prey is taken to a stump or lower branch to be eaten until the remainder of the carcass is light enough to carry.

ANATOMY 101

- The harpy eagle can grow up to 41 inches long with a wingspan of 6.5 feet!
- To catch their food, harpy eagles swoop down and grab their prey with their large hind talons, which are about 5 inches long.

BIRDWING BUTTERFLY

INSECT
Species: *Ornithoptera priamus*

Also known as: Cairns birdwing

Average wingspan: About 7 inches. The female's wingspan can reach nearly 8 inches.

Where it lives: Australia

Favorite food: Flower nectar

ANATOMY 101
- Like all butterflies, the birdwing sips nectar from flowers with its long, tubelike mouth.

Warning Spikes
The caterpillars of this butterfly eat the leaves of poisonous vines in the rainforest. Orange-red spines on their back warn birds that these caterpillars are a deadly meal!

This is the *largest* species of **butterfly** *found* in Australia.

The amazing *coloration* of this creature helps to **protect** it from *predators*.

In a "Flash"
When the blue morpho flaps its wings, the bright blue contrasts with the dull brown color, a phenomenon called "flashing." It makes it look like the butterfly is appearing and disappearing in the air. That's confusing to predators—and good for the blue morpho!

ANATOMY 101
- The top of this butterfly's wings aren't actually colored blue. The scales contain ridges that reflect blue light.
- The color underneath the wing is dull brown mixed with grays, blacks, and reds. When the butterfly sleeps at night it folds up its wings and blends into the foliage around it.

BLUE MORPHO BUTTERFLY

Species: *Morpho menelaus*

Average wingspan: About 6 inches

Where it lives: Tropical rainforests from Mexico to Colombia

Favorite food: The juices of rotting fruit

GLASSWING BUTTERFLY

This unusual *butterfly* has see-through **wings!**

INSECT
Species: *Greta oto*
Average wingspan: 2.2 to 2.3 inches
Where it lives: Central America

Some species of glasswing butterflies drink nectar from poisonous plants. This doesn't hurt the butterflies—but it does keep predators from eating them!

TAWNY OWL BUTTERFLY

These large *butterflies* can be easy to **spot** in the **rainforests** of *Central and South America.*

ANATOMY 101
- On the underside of each wing is a large yellow spot that looks like an owl's eye. Some scientists believe when predators see the spots, they think the butterfly is a type of poisonous tree frog and therefore choose to leave it alone.

INSECT
Species: *Caligo memnon*
Average wingspan: 6 to 8 inches
Where it lives: In Central and South America, from Mexico down to the Amazon basin

MONKEY-EATING EAGLE

Although it's called a monkey-eating eagle, flying lemurs are its favorite meal.

This *eagle*, the second-largest in the **world**, is also called the *Philippine Eagle*.

BIRD
Species: *Pithecophaga jefferyi*
Also known as: Philippine eagle
Average weight: About 17 pounds
Average wingspan: About 6.5 feet
Average length of body: 2.4 to 3.3 feet
Where it lives: Islands in the Philippines

Endangered

The monkey-eating eagle is only found in the Philippines and is the national bird of this country. These birds are becoming increasingly endangered because of losing most of their habitat to logging. There are fewer than 400 left in the wild today.

EAGLE OWL

This eagle owl *hunts* for prey in the **rainforests** of southeast *Asia*.

ANATOMY 101
- During the day, this owl stays concealed among the foliage of trees. But at night, it emerges, using its excellent night vision to hunt.

ANATOMY 101
- A shorter wingspan than other kinds of eagles helps this monkey-eating eagle maneuver through rainforest trees.

BIRD

Species: *Bubo nipalensis*

Also known as: Forest eagle owl, spot-bellied eagle owl

Where it lives: Southeast Asia

Dancing with the Birds

In some species of birds of paradise, the male will break out dance moves to attract a mate. The raggiana bird of paradise begins with some basic moves: hopping around from leg to leg, flapping its wings, and shaking its orange tail feathers. His show peaks when he hops onto a tree branch to puff out the feathers on his "cape" to show off.

BIRD
Species: *Paradisaea raggiana*
Average length of body: 13 to 14 inches
Where it lives: Eastern New Guinea

ANATOMY 101
- People in Papua New Guinea use these birds' plumes
  (or feathers) to decorate their ceremonial costumes.
- The yellow-striped feathers on the male's neck are shaped like a fan or cape.

These birds dine on flowers that grow in the rainforest treetops.

RAGGIANA
BIRD OF PARADISE

BLUE BIRD OF PARADISE

This *beautiful bird* lives in a small area of **Papua New Guinea.**

There are more than 30 species of birds of paradise in rainforests in Indonesia, Papua New Guinea, and Australia.

Legendary Birds

The feathers of these birds were brought to Spain in 1522 by explorers and given to the king as a gift. The people of Spain thought the feathers were too beautiful to come from birds who lived in forests. They had to be from paradise! That's how these birds got their name.

BIRD
Species: *Paradisaea rudolphi*
Average length of body: About 12 inches
Where it lives: Southeastern New Guinea

45

Glossary

amphibian: a cold-blooded animal with a backbone that spends part of its life in water, and part on land

canopy: a tall layer of trees in the rainforest that acts as a roof over the lower layers

carnivorous: a living thing that feeds on animals

emergent layer: the top layer of a rainforest

foliage: the leaves of plants or trees

forage: to search for food

habitat: the place where an animal or plant lives

mammal: a warm-blooded animal with a backbone that feeds milk to its young and usually has hair on its skin

predator: an animal that hunts other animals for food

prehensile: a kind of tail that can grab things, the way a hand can

prey: an animal hunted for food

rainforest: a warm, wet forest that is home to millions of plants and animals and gets more than 70 inches of rainfall a year, on average

reptile: a cold-blooded animal with a backbone that lives on land

territory: an area of land that a group of animals or people claim as their home

understory: a layer of plants and small trees that grow underneath the rainforest canopy

Forests of the World

The *green* areas on this map indicate where the world's great forests — including tropical *rainforests* — are located.

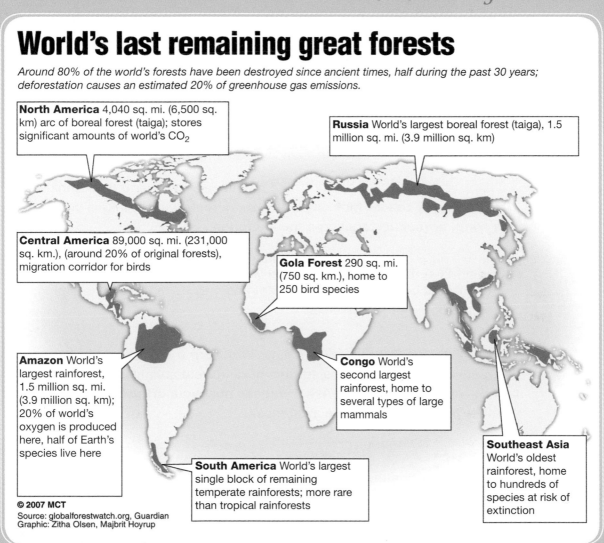

World's last remaining great forests

Around 80% of the world's forests have been destroyed since ancient times, half during the past 30 years; deforestation causes an estimated 20% of greenhouse gas emissions.

North America 4,040 sq. mi. (6,500 sq. km) arc of boreal forest (taiga); stores significant amounts of world's CO_2

Russia World's largest boreal forest (taiga), 1.5 million sq. mi. (3.9 million sq. km)

Central America 89,000 sq. mi. (231,000 sq. km.), (around 20% of original forests), migration corridor for birds

Gola Forest 290 sq. mi. (750 sq. km.), home to 250 bird species

Amazon World's largest rainforest, 1.5 million sq. mi. (3.9 million sq. km); 20% of world's oxygen is produced here, half of Earth's species live here

Congo World's second largest rainforest, home to several types of large mammals

Southeast Asia World's oldest rainforest, home to hundreds of species at risk of extinction

South America World's largest single block of remaining temperate rainforests; more rare than tropical rainforests

© 2007 MCT
Source: globalforestwatch.org, Guardian
Graphic: Zitha Olsen, Majbrit Hoyrup

PROTECT PLANET EARTH,
It's the Only One We've Got . . .

Here are some ways you can help.

1. Learn All You Can! Read books and visit websites to learn about what's happening in the rainforest. (www.loveearth.com)

2. Spread the Word. The next time you have to do a book report or project in school, pick one with a rainforest theme. Make a poster, write a song, or read a story about the rainforest.

3. Use Less Paper. Trees are used to make paper. Try to reduce the amount you use. Save paper that has only been used on one side, and use the back for scrap paper.

4. Create an Art Gallery. With your friends or classmates, create paintings or clay sculptures of rainforest animals. Make signs with facts about each animal. Ask if you can post your art gallery in a school or other public place to raise awareness.

5. Shop Smart. Ask your parents to shop for products that weren't made by hurting the rainforest. Look online for responsible ways to buy products like coffee, bananas, and wood.